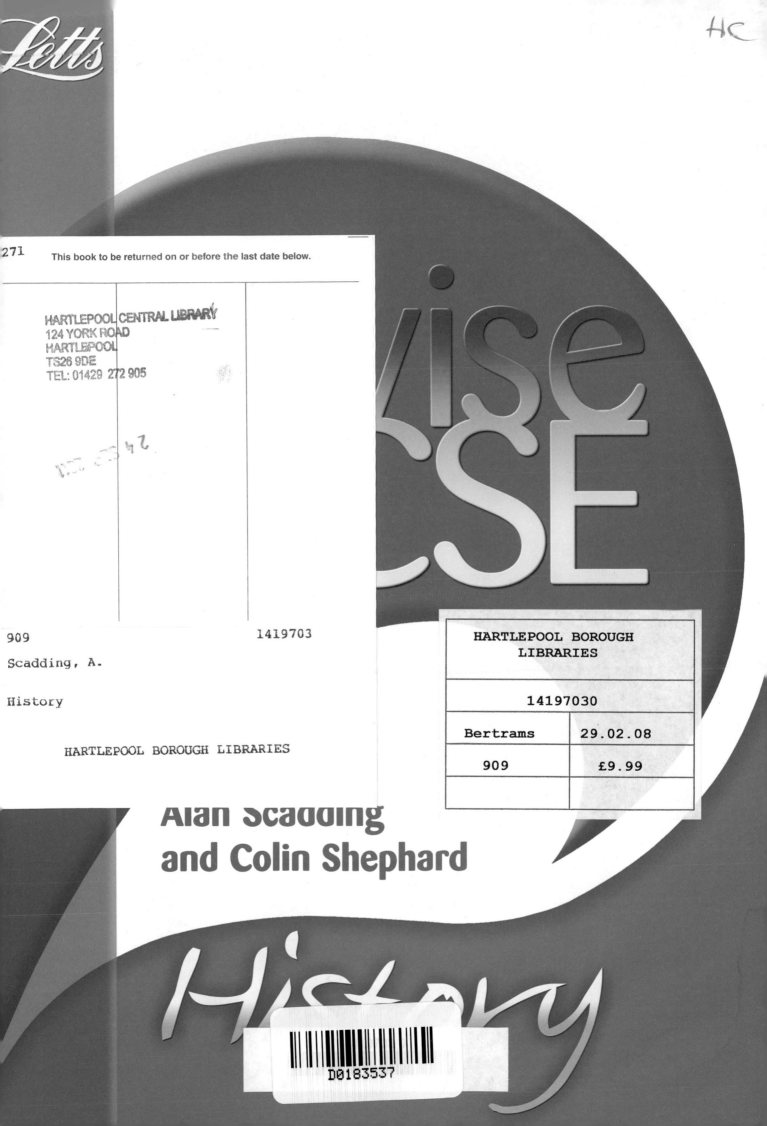

HC

Letts

271

vise
SE

Alan Scadding
and Colin Shephard

History

D0183537

Contents

Britain 1906–1918

The First World War 1914–1918

The peace settlements

The League of Nations

Hitler's foreign policy

The Second World War 1939–1945

The causes of the Cold War 1945–1949

Tension and détente 1950–1981

The collapse of communism

Britain 1919–1951

Russia 1914–1941

Germany 1918–1945

The USA 1919–1941

This book and your GCSE course

	AQA B	EDEXCEL A	OCR B
Syllabus number	3042	1334	1937
Terminal papers	2 x 105 min. papers, each 37.5%	1 x 120 min. paper 40% 1 x 105 min. paper 35%	1 x 120 min. paper 45% 1 x 90 min. paper 30%
Coursework	25%	25%	25%
		SPECIFICATION REFERENCE NUMBERS	
Britain 1906-1918	Paper 1 Section B Part 7 Paper 2 Option D		Paper 2 Brit Depth Study
The First World War 1914-1918		Paper 2 B2	
The peace settlements 1919-1923	Paper 1 Section A Part 2		Paper 1 Core KQ1
The League of Nations	Paper 1 Section A Part 2		Paper 1 Core KQ2
Hitler's foreign policy 1933-1939	Paper 1 Section A Part 3		Paper 1 Core KQ3
The Second World War 1939-1945	Paper 1 Option V and Z	Paper 2 B5	
The causes of the Cold War 1945-1949	Paper 1 Section A Part 4	Paper 1 A6	Paper 1 Core KQ4
Tension and détente 1950-1981	Paper 1 Section A Part 5, Paper 3 Section B Part 6 Option D	Paper 1 A6, Paper 2 B7	Paper 1 Core KQ5
The collapse of communism 1956-1991	Paper 1 Section A Part 6	Paper 1 A6	Paper 1 Core KQ6
Britain 1919-1952	Paper 1 Section B Part 8 Paper 2 Option D		
Russia 1914-1941	Paper 2 Option A	Paper 1 A4, Paper 2 B1	Paper 1 Depth Study B
Germany 1918-1945	Paper 2 Option B	Paper 2 B4	Paper 1 Depth Study A
The USA 1919-1941	Paper 2 Option C	Paper 2 B3	Paper 1 Depth Study C

4

Visit your awarding body for full details of your course or download your complete GCSE specifications.

STAY YOUR COURSE!

Use these pages to get to know your course
- Make sure you know your exam board
- Check which specification and option you are doing

- Know how your course is assessed:
  - What format are the papers?
  - How is coursework assessed?
  - How many papers are there?

	WJEC A	WJEC B	NICCEA
	165	*165*	
	1 x 120 min. 45%	1 x 120 min. 45%	1 x 120 min. paper 40%
	1 x 75 min. 30%	1 x 75 min. 30%	1 x 90 min. paper 35%
	25%	25%	25%
SPECIFICATION REFERENCE NUMBERS			
	Paper 1 Depth Study 3		
	Paper 1 Depth Study 3		
			Paper 1 A1
			Paper 1 B1
			Paper 2
			Paper 2
			Paper 2
	Paper 1 Depth Study 4	Paper 1 Depth Study 4	
	Paper 1 Depth Study 5, Paper 2 Outline Study 3		Paper 1 A2
	Paper 1 Depth Study 7, Paper 2 Outline Study 1	Paper 1 Depth Study 3	Paper 1 A1
	Paper 1 Depth Study 6, Paper 2 Outline Study 4		Paper 1 A3

Preparing for the examination

Successful revision

The final three months before taking your GCSE examination are very important in achieving your best grade.

- **Go through the list of topics** in your Examination Board's specification and identify those that you feel you need to concentrate on.
- Try not to spend valuable time on topics you already know. It makes you feel good but does not move you forward.
- Study each topic carefully. Mark up the text by **underlining**, **highlighting** or **making notes**.
- **Ask questions**: Why? How? What happened next? You will get ideas for these questions from past examination papers.
- Then make your own **revision note summary** of the main points. Use bullet points, mind maps and patterned notes.
- Keep your revision notes **organised**.
- One of the best ways to revise is to **answer the type of questions you will get in the examination**. These will require you to use what you know – this helps you to memorise things better.

How this book will help you

Letts Revise GCSE Modern British and World History Study Guide will help you because:

- it contains all the **essential content** for your GCSE course
- it contains **Progress Checks** and GCSE questions to help you confirm your understanding
- it gives **sample GCSE questions** with answers and advice from an examiner on how to improve
- the questions in this book have been written by experienced examiners who are writing the questions for 2003 and beyond
- the summary table on pages 4–5 gives you a quick reference guide to the requirements for your examination
- **margin comments** and **highlighted key points** will draw to your attention important things you might otherwise miss

Five ways to improve your grade

1 Answer the question that is set

Some students fail to answer the actual question set. Perhaps they misread the question or answer a different question that they had prepared for. **Read the question once right through and then again more slowly**. Some students **underline the key words** in a question. Make sure you do not just write everything you know about the topic. **Only include information if it supports your answer** to the question set. Examiners do not award marks for correct information that is not relevant to the question. If there is a choice of questions, **make sure you can answer all parts of the question** before choosing to tackle it.

2 Think carefully about the length of your answer

You should **use the number of marks allocated to the question as a guide to how much you need to write**. Questions that carry 2 or 3 marks require no more than 2 or 3 lines of answer. Remember, no matter how much you write you will never score more than 2 or 3 marks. Questions that carry 8, 10 or more marks require extended writing with points being explained.

3 Questions based on historical sources

Some of the questions will be based on historical source material. **Make sure you use the source in your answer**. You will also need to use your knowledge of the topic to help you explain what the source means and whether the source can be trusted. Only include this knowledge if it helps you to say something better about the sources.

4 Explaining, analysing and making judgements

Questions that ask for extended writing will also require you to produce explanations. These questions often ask why something happened. Make sure you give several reasons, and that you **explain how those reasons helped bring about a particular event or development**. Some questions require you to reach a judgement, e.g. whether one cause was more important than another. You must **support your judgement with evidence**.

5 Quality of written communication

In those questions that require extended writing, marks are awarded for the quality of your written communication. This includes **explaining** you arguments clearly, **organising** your answers carefully, and **using correct grammar, punctuation and spelling**.

Internet links

Try these for revision. Many are very good general sites, which keep links up-to-date. All cover an aspect of the Modern World History course.

General	History Resources. Some very good links on many subjects.	http://www.liv.ac.uk/~evansjon/humanities/history/history.html
	Spartacus International. Good for the First World War and Vietnam. Good links to other sites.	http://www.spartacus.schoolnet.co.uk
	Internet Sourcebooks. A guide about how to research on the Internet, with very useful links.	http://www.fordham.edu/halsall
	Historical Text Archive. Good links on many subjects. Look under Europe.	http://historicaltextarchive.com/
	The Imperial War Museum site. Look for recollections of soldiers in the First World War, the Holocaust etc.	http://www.iwm.org.uk/lambeth/lambeth.htm
	The History Channel. An excellent historical search engine.	http://www.historychannel.com/index.html
Britain	Primary Documents about the United Kingdom, many of them about the 20th Century.	http://library.byu.edu/~rdh/eurodocs/uk.html
Britain	Guardian Century. Easy access to articles on important events.	http://www.guardiancentury.co.uk
Cold War	Cold War International History Project. An archive of Cold War Documents, with many links to other sites.	http://cwihp.si.edu/default.htm
Germany	Holocaust Cybrary. Links and information for teachers.	http://www.remember.org/educate
Northern Ireland	Northern Ireland CAIN Project. A very comprehensive site on Northern Ireland.	http://cain.ulst.ac.uk/
Russia	Chronology of Russian History. Useful chronology with effective notes.	http://www.departments.bucknell.edu/russian/chrono.html
Russia	Russian History. Links on the Revolution, the Second World War and the Cold War.	http://www.departments.bucknell.edu/russian/history.html
Russia	Russian and East European History, Geography and Sociology.	gopher://gopher.tamu.edu/00/.data/soviet.exhibit.intro
Russia	The Russian Revolution. The Revolution and the period afterwards.	http://www.barnsdle.demon.co.uk/russ/rusrev.html
First World War	Trenches on the Web. The first and best First World War site.	http://www.worldwar1.com/index.html
First World War	First World War Flying Aces. An excellent site with everything to do with aircraft.	http://www.theaerodrome.com
First World War	World War One Document Archive. This does more than it says, for example there is a good collection of photographs.	http://www.lib.byu.edu/~rdh/wwi/
Second World War	Second World War, a British focus	http://www.warlinks.com/

Britain 1906–1918

The following topics are covered in this chapter:

- The Liberal reforms 1906–1914
- Votes for women
- The Home Front during the First World War

1.1 The Liberal reforms 1906–1914

LEARNING SUMMARY

After studying this section you will know:

- attitudes towards poverty at the end of the nineteenth century
- why the Liberal Government passed so many reforms to help the poor
- the reforms passed by the Liberal Government
- the different views about how effective these reforms were
- how the 'People's Budget' of 1909 led to the reform of the House of Lords

Attitudes towards poverty

AQA B
OCR B
WJEC A

The phrase **self-help** came from a very popular Victorian book of the same name. It meant that people should work hard and support themselves and their families, and not depend on help from others.

Laissez-faire means that governments should interfere in people's lives as little as possible. People should be given as much freedom as possible. This meant that it was not the government's job to help people who were poor, sick or old.

Towards the end of the nineteenth century attitudes towards poverty began to change. For much of the Victorian period many people had believed in **self-help** and **laissez-faire**. These attitudes can be summed up as follows.

- If people were poor it was their own fault. Poverty was caused by idleness or wasting money on drink.
- People ought to be able to support themselves and their family without help from anyone else.
- It was not the job of the state to help people just because they were poor.

Of course, there were workhouses for the poor but these were harsh places designed to encourage people to support themselves. The conditions in the workhouse were meant to be worse than those in which the poorest workers were living outside the workhouse. Families were split up, discipline was harsh and the food was dreadful. Many workhouses were like vast prisons.

KEY POINT

At the beginning of the twentieth century many people thought it was your own fault if you were poor and that the government should not help you.

Fig. 1.1 Dinner in the St Marylebone Workhouse in about 1900.

Although workhouses were responsible for looking after the poor, there were many other voluntary organisations providing help.

- Dr Barnardo's Homes for destitute children. The first one was set up in 1866 and by 1900 there were over 100.
- Churches and charities set up homes for the homeless. The London Congregational Union, for example, had a home for men in London's docklands. By six o'clock every night there was a queue of 500–600 men trying to get in.

Useful as the work of these charities was it could not cope with the scale of poverty in 1900. Attitudes had to be changed so the state could do something to alleviate poverty.

Reasons why reforms were passed

AQA B
OCR B
WJEC A

1. Two individuals were important in bringing to everyone's attention the scale of poverty at that time.

Charles Booth

Booth was a rich businessman who moved to London in 1880. He was appalled by the slums he saw in the East End of London and decided to gather evidence that would persuade other people that something had to be done. His investigators visited every house in the area and asked detailed questions. His first report was published in 1889. It showed that one-third of London's population was living in appalling poverty. Booth also identified the main causes of poverty: old age, sickness, unemployment and low wages, not idleness or drink. In all Booth published 17 volumes of evidence between 1898 and 1903.

> Booth and Rowntree collected evidence about poverty which could be used to support their arguments.

Seebohm Rowntree

Rowntree was the son of a wealthy chocolate manufacturer in York. He had read Booth's report and decided to do a similar survey in York. His book, *Poverty, a Study of Town Life,* showed that about one-third of the population lived in poverty. Rowntree claimed that the main causes of poverty were that the family's wage earner was ill, old or dead and that wages were too low.

These reports made clear:

- the scale of poverty in Britain
- that it was too widespread for charities to cope with and the government would have to act
- that poverty was not caused by idleness, spending money on drink or gambling

> The conclusions of Booth and Rowntree about the causes of poverty differed from the accepted views of the time.

2. Attitudes towards poverty were changing in the Liberal Party. The Liberals came to power in 1905, and in 1906 won a big victory in the general election. The Liberals were divided into two groups:

- those who supported the traditional Liberal values of self-help and laissez-faire
- those who supported '**New Liberalism**'. They were convinced by the work of Booth and Rowntree that the government had to do something about poverty. They accepted that the main causes of poverty were illness, old age, low wages and unemployment.

3. Some Liberals were influenced by the ideas of the small, but growing Labour Party. In 1900, the Independent Labour Party, some trade unions and some socialist societies met and agreed to form a new party called the Labour Representation Committee. In 1906 it became the Labour Party, with 52 MPs. It was obviously winning support from the working classes and some Liberals were worried that, unless they changed their policies on poverty and social reform, they would lose even more support to the Labour Party.

4. **David Lloyd George** was the leading force behind many of these reforms. Between 1908 and 1915 he was Chancellor of the Exchequer in the Liberal Government. This meant he was in charge of the country's finances and had the money and the power to carry the reforms through. He was a 'New Liberal' and believed the government had a responsibility to look after the poor. The other important 'New Liberal' in the government was **Winston Churchill**. These two men worked hard to get the reforms through.

Examiner's tip: You will need to be able to explain why reforms to help the poor started to be passed at this time.

5. In 1900 it was discovered that 40 per cent of the men volunteering for the army (to fight in the Boer War in South Africa) were unfit to join. In most cases this was because they were suffering from malnutrition. This shocked many people.

The Liberal reforms

AQA B
OCR B
WJEC A

The Children's Charter

Fig. 1.2

The Children's Charter is the name given to a series of laws helping children.

- 1906 School Meals Act. Local education authorities were given the power to give free meals to poor children and cheap meals to other children.

- 1907 The School Medical Service. Regular medical inspections in schools were started. Free medical treatment for poor children could be provided by the local education authority.

- 1908 The Children's Act. Children were banned from public houses, and not allowed to beg. Selling cigarettes to children was made illegal. Child offenders were to be sent to special juvenile courts and borstals rather than to adult courts and prisons.

Helping the old

Fig. 1.3

One of the main causes of poverty was old age. Many old people had no choice but to go into workhouse. The introduction of the old age pension in 1908 changed that.

- Anyone over the age of 70 with an annual income of under £21 a year was paid a pension of 25p a week.
- People with an income of over £21 a year received a reduced pension.

Helping the unemployed

Fig. 1.4

Another major cause of poverty was unemployment.

- 1909 Employment exchanges were set up to help people find jobs.

- 1909 Minimum wages were fixed for people working in the 'sweated industries' where there were no trade unions.

- 1911 Health insurance. To insure some workers who earned less than £160 a year, workers, employers and the government paid a weekly amount into a fund. From this fund workers were given benefits such as free medical treatment and sickness benefit of 50p a week for up to six months if unable to work because of illness.

- 1911 Unemployment insurance. In trades like building and shipbuilding where seasonal employment was common (at certain times of the year people were often laid off), unemployment benefits of 35p a week were paid for up to 15 weeks a year. Both the workers and the employers paid a weekly amount for this. In those trades covered by the scheme it was compulsory to belong. About 4 million workers were covered by the scheme.

These reforms might seem impressive but note their limitations given in Point of view No. 2 on page 13.

Judgements on the reforms

Historians disagree about how important these reforms were.

Point of view No. 1

The reforms were very important.

- These reforms were the beginning of the **welfare state**.
  They established the principle that the government had a responsibility to look after people who were poor. Although the schemes did not help all poor people, further reforms would inevitably follow now that the principle had been established. (For example, in 1936 health insurance was extended to farmworkers and domestic servants.)

- These reforms did recognise that poverty was due to factors like low wages, sickness and unemployment, and they did try to begin to do something about these.

- The reforms did help a lot of people. The worst examples of poverty were dealt with.

- Even these limited reforms were strongly opposed by many people. If the Liberals had tried to pass more extensive reforms they might have been defeated. It was better to make a start than do nothing.

Point of view No. 2

When you look at the reforms in detail they are not as impressive as they first seem.

- The reforms only helped the very poor, and only some of them. For example, old age pensions were only for those with an income below £21 a year; health insurance was not for women workers or other groups like farmworkers. Unemployment insurance was only for those in certain trades. In 1906 local education authorities were only given the power to provide free or cheap meals; they did not have to do so.

- The Poor Law was not reformed so many poor people still had to go into workhouses.

> **Examiner's tip:**
> You must know these different arguments. You should also decide which one you agree with.

Paying for the reforms

AQA B
OCR B
WJEC A

Even if the reforms were just a beginning they still had to be paid for. Lloyd George was determined that the rich would pay for them.

The People's Budget

In 1910 he introduced a budget that came to be known as the '**People's Budget**'. In this he planned to:

- increase income tax for the rich
- impose a supertax on the very rich
- impose a tax on the increased value of land when it was sold

The budget had to be passed by the House of Commons and the House of Lords. The Liberals had a huge majority in the Commons but they ran into problems with the Lords.

> **The House of Lords was very angry about the Land Tax because most of its members owned a lot of land and would have to pay the tax.**

The reform of the House of Lords

The House of Lords consisted largely of hereditary peers. They had not been elected by anyone, most of them were Conservatives, and many were rich landowners. They disliked Lloyd George's budget because they would be the ones paying the increased taxes. Many of them were also opposed to many of the reforms because they believed that people should look after themselves and not depend on the government.

KEY POINT

> The House of Lords was not elected. Its members were there because they had inherited titles from their fathers. Liberals said the Lords had no right to delay reforms being passed by the House of Commons which was elected.

Fig. 1.5 A cartoon published in 1912. What point do you think the cartoonist is making about Lloyd George's reforms?

The House of Lords rejected the budget. This caused a storm because it was accepted that the Lords would not reject bills that were to do with money. Why should the Lords who were not elected be allowed to reject bills from the House of Commons which was elected?

The following events then took place.

1. In 1910 the Liberal Government called a general election which it won narrowly.
2. The House of Lords accepted the budget.
3. The Liberals had decided the House of Lords must be reformed and so called another general election in 1910 over the issue of Lords' reform. The Liberals again just won.
4. In 1911 the Parliament Bill (to reform the Lords) was passed by the House of Commons. It then went to the House of Lords. The government threatened to create 500 new Liberal Lords to get the bill through the House of Lords.
5. The House of Lords passed the Parliament Act in 1911.

- The House of Lords could not reject bills about money.
- The Lords could only delay other bills for two years. They would then become law.
- There would now be general elections at least every five years.

Payment for MPs

One other important reform the Liberal Government passed in 1911 was that MPs were paid for the first time. They were given £400 a year. This was to allow working men to become MPs.

PROGRESS CHECK

1. Write down four reasons why the Liberal Government started to pass social reforms.
2. List five important social reforms passed by the Liberals.
3. Name two criticisms of these reforms.
4. Describe the content of Lloyd George's 'People's Budget'.
5. How were the powers of the House of Lords reduced?

1. The work of Booth and Rowntree. The ideas of the 'New Liberals'. Volunteers for the army to fight in the Boer War were not fit. To stop the Labour Party winning the support of the working classes. 2. Old age pensions, insurance against unemployment, insurance against sickness, free school meals for the poor, medical inspections of children at school 3. Old age pensions were only given to the very poor. Local education authorities did not have to provide free meals for poor children. 4. It put up income tax for the rich. It introduced a supertax for the very rich. It introduced a new tax on land. 5. It was not allowed to reject bills which were concerned with money. It could hold up other bills for just two years.

1.2 Votes for women

LEARNING SUMMARY

After studying this section you will know:

- the position of women in 1900
- the aims, leaders, methods and effectiveness of the suffragists
- the aims, leaders, methods and effectiveness of the suffragettes
- the arguments used for and against giving women the vote
- the work women did in the war
- why some women were given the vote in 1918

The position of women in 1900

AQA B
OCR B
WJEC A

In 1900 women were still second-class citizens although the situation was improving:

- 1878   London University allowed women to take degrees on the same terms as men
- 1870s   Women qualified as doctors
- 1882   The Married Women's Property Act allowed women to own property after they married
- 1886   The Guardianship of Children Act allowed women to claim custody of their children if the marriage broke up

The position of women in terms of political rights was a mixed one:

- 1888   Unmarried women were allowed to vote in some local elections
- 1894   Women were allowed to vote in local elections and to stand as candidates

KEY POINT

Demands for women to be given the vote in general elections grew around 1900 because they could now vote in local elections and because of the advances they had made in other areas.

At the end of the nineteenth century, women were still not allowed to vote in elections for Parliament, nor were they allowed to become MPs. The campaign for women to be allowed to vote began in the 1850s. By the 1870s there were **suffrage** societies all over the country. The campaigners were mostly middle-class women. Even so, by 1900 only a minority of people in Britain thought that women should have the vote. Feelings were strong on both sides.

The Suffragists

AQA B
OCR B
WJEC A

> The Suffragists believed in lawful, peaceful methods.

In 1897 **Mrs Millicent Garrett Fawcett** formed the **National Union of Women's Suffrage Societies** (NUWSS) from the hundreds of suffrage groups all over the country. The members of the NUWSS were known as **Suffragists**.

Aims

The Suffragists did not demand the vote for all women. They wanted women to have the vote on the same terms as men at the time. Only about 60 per cent of men had the vote.

Fig. 1.6 A poster published in 1910. Is it supporting or attacking the idea of women being given the vote?

Methods

The NUWSS believed in using peaceful methods such as: reasoned argument; holding meetings; issuing leaflets; and collecting petitions. They met with politicians and argued their case. During elections they supported candidates who were in favour of votes for women. The NUWSS trained women to speak at public meetings. In the 1906 election they put up male candidates to compete with Liberal politicians who were opposed to votes for women. In 1907 the organisation held its first march in London (known as the 'Mud March' because of the weather). Over 3,000 women marched. Many people were shocked at seeing women marching in public.

> Don't forget the Suffragists! They were just as important as the Suffragettes and kept winning support for the cause of votes for women right up to the beginning of the First World War.

The Suffragists did not regard their work as an attack on men but as a reform for the good of everyone. They wanted to convert public opinion. They did not want to antagonise men, but to convince them of the sense of their arguments.

Under Mrs Fawcett's leadership their numbers grew rapidly and they won a lot of support. They were very well organised. The NUWSS had full-time paid organisers who co-ordinated activities across the country. In 1910 they collected a petition of 280,000 signatures.

At first the NUWSS and the WSPU (Women's Social and Political Union, see page 17) worked well together but Mrs Fawcett grew worried about the violent methods of the Suffragettes. She thought they were losing the movement support with the public and MPs. The NUWSS worked hard to win back public support and by 1914 it had more than 100,000 members.

The Suffragettes

AQA B
OCR B
WJEC A

In 1903 **Mrs Emmeline Pankhurst**, helped by her two daughters Christabel and Sylvia, formed the **Women's Social and Political Union** (WSPU). Mrs Pankhurst was a member of the Manchester Suffrage Society and the Labour Party. However:

- she grew tired of the lukewarm attitude of the Labour Party towards votes for women and left
- she became disappointed with the new Liberal Government. Several attempts were made in the House of Commons to give women the vote between 1906 and 1912 but they were all defeated because the government refused to provide support. Asquith, who became Prime Minister in 1908, was not in favour of votes for women, although other ministers, like Lloyd George, were sympathetic
- she became impatient with the fact that the Suffragists' moderate methods had failed to achieve reform.

> **Examiner's tip:**
> Be ready to compare the aims and the methods of the Suffragists and the Suffragettes.

Fig. 1.7 A poster published for the 1910 election. It shows a Suffragette being force-fed.

Aims

The Suffragettes wanted women to have the vote on the same basis as men. They also wanted reforms to improve social conditions and believed that if women had the vote they would be able to put pressure on the government to carry these out.

Methods

The Suffragettes believed in '**Deeds not Words**' and when it became clear that the new Liberal Government was not going to introduce reform, they turned to militant methods. They also restricted membership of the WSPU to women: men were not allowed to join. They soon showed that they would be using different methods from the NUWSS. In 1905 Christabel Pankhurst was sent to prison for hitting and spitting at a policeman at a Liberal meeting. However, for a time their methods were similar to the Suffragists. One of the most effective was to use megaphones to heckle Liberal candidates at by-elections.

In 1908 **Asquith** took over as Prime Minister. He challenged the NUWSS and the WSPU to prove that there was a widespread demand for votes for women. In response both organisations held large marches in London. Trains brought hundreds of thousands of women to London for the demonstrations. However, at the WSPU march stones were thrown at the windows of the Prime Minister's house in Downing Street. The women responsible were sent to prison – but to their fellow suffragettes, they were heroines. This was the turning point. With the government finding excuses for not granting women the vote, the Suffragettes stepped up their violent methods.

- In 1908 a group of Suffragettes tried to break their way into the House of Commons – they were sentenced to three months in prison.
- In 1909 Suffragettes smashed government office buildings – 108 women were arrested.
- Once in prison, the Suffragettes went on **hunger strike**. The authorities could not afford to let the women die and they released them. Later, the authorities changed their tactics and began to force-feed women who would not eat. This involved putting a tube down the women's throat and pouring food in. It was very unpleasant. Some Suffragettes barricaded themselves into their cells in an attempt to avoid force-feeding.

The Conciliation Bill

The NUWSS continued to co-operate with the government over the Conciliation Bill but the Suffragettes lost patience and returned to their violent tactics.

In 1910 the government introduced a Conciliation Bill to give votes to women. Both the NUWSS and the WSPU were involved in drawing it up. The WSPU even called a truce for a time and suspended its violence. However, the government kept finding excuses for not letting the Bill become law and at the end of 1911 the patience of the Suffragettes ran out.

- In 1911 the WSPU started a window smashing campaign. Thousands of pounds of damage was done and hundreds of Suffragettes were sent to prison. They organised a mass hunger strike in prisons all over the country.
- The campaign of violence continued into 1912 and 1913: public buildings were bombed; chemicals were poured into postboxes and thousands of letters destroyed; telephone wires were cut.
- Lloyd George's house was damaged by a bomb. Mrs Pankhurst received a three-year prison sentence for this.
- In 1913 Emily Davison threw herself in front of the King's horse at the Derby and was killed.

It was called the 'Cat and Mouse Act' because it was thought the government was playing with the Suffragettes in the same way as a cat plays with a mouse: appearing to let it escape, then catching it again.

- The **Cat and Mouse Act** 1913 was introduced. Force-feeding was unpopular with the public so the government introduced the Cat and Mouse Act. This allowed the government to release hunger strikers from prison but re-arrest and return them to prison whenever it wanted. However, it did not stop the violence or the hunger strikes.
- Then in August 1914 the whole situation changed when Britain declared war on Germany and the First World War began.

By the beginning of the First World War people in Britain were still divided over whether women should have the vote. Here is a summary of the arguments used by the two sides.

Arguments for giving women the vote

1. In the late nineteenth century women had gained many legal rights making them equal with men. Women were taking up new jobs, e.g. as doctors, but the one way in which they were not equal was that they could not vote.
2. Some women had been given the right to vote in local elections, so why not in national elections?
3. Women were gaining the vote in other countries, e.g. New Zealand, Australia, and parts of the USA, so why not in Britain?
4. Giving women the vote would lead to more social reforms being passed. This would benefit many poor people.

Arguments against giving women the vote

1. If the vote was given to all women they would outnumber men, because only 60 per cent of men had the vote: male voters had to be householders living in the constituency for one year.
2. Women were emotional creatures and were not capable of making important political decisions.
3. If women became involved in politics they would neglect their duties at home as wives and mothers.
4. A woman's brain was different from a man's and was not suitable for making political decisions.
5. The behaviour of the Suffragettes proved that women were not sensible enough to be given the vote.
6. Liberals feared that giving the vote only to women with property might benefit the Conservatives.
7. Conservatives feared that most women would vote for the Liberals, or even the new Labour Party.

> Some of these reasons against giving women the vote were purely party political ones. No party wanted to do something that would give the other parties more voters.

Judgements on the methods of the Suffragettes

AQA B
OCR B
WJEC A

Historians disagree over whether the Suffragettes' methods were counter-productive. Here are some of the arguments they put forward.

In support of Suffragette methods	Against Suffragette methods
• The NUWSS had been campaigning for some years but had never achieved the publicity that the Suffragettes got. • The Suffragette methods brought the issue of votes for women to everyone's attention. Otherwise it might have been ignored. • The Suffragettes had made sure that once the war was over the issue of votes for women would return. They had made sure it would not go away. It was now inevitable that women would be given the vote some time.	• They gave Asquith the excuse he needed not to give women the vote. • The government could not be seen to give in to violence because if it did other groups (like the Irish) would resort to violence. • They convinced many people that women were not 'sensible' enough to be trusted with the vote. • The Liberals had at long last accepted the principle of votes for women and it is probable that they would have passed a Bill in 1913. However, the extremism of the Suffragettes disgusted many Liberal MPs, who now turned against the idea.

Women in the First World War

AQA B
OCR B
WJEC A

As soon as the First World War began both the NUWSS and the WSPU ended their campaigns. Helping Britain win the war was their first duty. Mrs Fawcett and Mrs Pankhurst both campaigned for women to help the war effort.

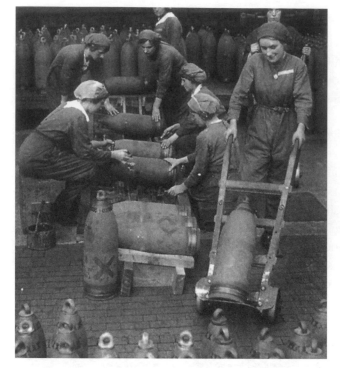

So many men had gone away to fight that women were needed to do their jobs in factories and on farms. By 1915 Britain was facing a serious shortage of shells and bullets because there were not enough men to work in **munitions** factories.

In 1915 the government drew up a register of women who were available for work. Over 100,000 were on the register, but only 5,000 were given jobs. This was because many men workers, the trade unions and factory owners were against having women in factories. They claimed they were unskilled and would not be able to do the work properly. They were also worried about women accepting lower wages than men and taking men's jobs away from them.

The situation changed in 1916 when conscription was introduced. This made it clear to everyone that women workers were needed.

Fig. 1.8 A photograph of women working in a munitions factory during the First World War.

> You need to start thinking now about why women were given the vote in 1918. Was it because of the activities of the Suffragists and Suffragettes, or because of the way in which women contributed to the War effort?

By the end of the War women were working in all sorts of jobs. Many involved heavy work which people would have thought women incapable of before the War. The women learned new skills quickly and often ended up doing the work better than the men they had replaced.

Keeping Britain fed

Fig. 1.9 A painting of a land girl ploughing.

Farmers were also suspicious at first of unskilled women working on their farms. However, as more and more labourers went to fight they were gradually persuaded to accept women. By 1917, when the German submarine blockade was at its worst, Britain was seriously short of food. An extra 2.5 million acres of land were ploughed and workers were needed for this work and for the harvest. The **Women's Land Army** was formed to do this work. By 1918 16,000 women had joined. They did a crucial job in keeping Britain fed.

Keeping Britain armed and equipped

Here are some of the places women worked:

- munitions factories
- surface work at coal mines
- engineering
- banks
- buses and railways
- gasworks
- near the battlefront and at home as nurses

Gaining the vote in 1918

AQA B
OCR B
WJEC A

- By the end of the war women, through their work in the war, had changed many people's ideas about their role in society. They had showed that they were not weak, fragile and stupid. They had played a crucial part in winning the war. Even people like Asquith, who had opposed women getting the vote, had changed his mind.

- In 1916 Lloyd George had replaced Asquith as Prime Minister. He was far more sympathetic towards women getting the vote.

- The government realised that men who were away fighting had lost their right to vote. This was because you had to be living in Britain to qualify to vote. It was clear that the law had to be changed and this gave the government the opportunity to give women the vote too.

In 1918 the **Representation of the People Act** was passed. This gave the vote to:

- women aged 30 and over (in the 1918 general election 8.5 million women were able to vote)

- men aged 21 and over

It also allowed women to stand for election as MPs.

Women were not given the vote on the same basis as men because

- if women had the vote at 21, they would have outnumbered men voters

- many people felt that women in their twenties were too silly and not responsible enough to have the vote

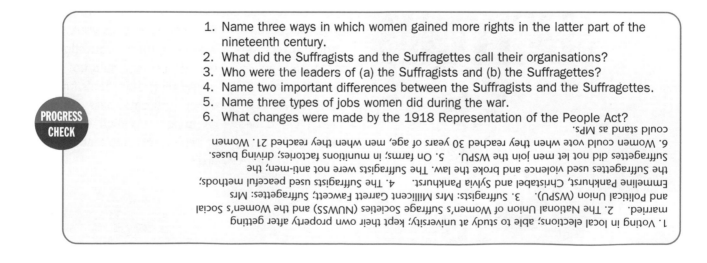

PROGRESS
CHECK

1. Name three ways in which women gained more rights in the latter part of the nineteenth century.
2. What did the Suffragists and the Suffragettes call their organisations?
3. Who were the leaders of (a) the Suffragists and (b) the Suffragettes?
4. Name two important differences between the Suffragists and the Suffragettes.
5. Name three types of jobs women did during the war.
6. What changes were made by the 1918 Representation of the People Act?

1. Voting in local elections; able to study at university; kept their own property after getting married. 2. The National Union of Women's Suffrage Societies (NUWSS) and the Women's Social and Political Union (WSPU). 3. Suffragists: Mrs Millicent Garrett Fawcett; Suffragettes: Mrs Emmeline Pankhurst, Christabel and Sylvia Pankhurst. 4. The Suffragists used peaceful methods; the Suffragettes used violence and broke the law. The Suffragists were not anti-men; the Suffragettes did not let men join the WSPU. 5. On farms; in munitions factories; driving buses. 6. Women could vote when they reached 30 years of age, men when they reached 21. Women could stand as MPs.

1.3 The Home Front during the First World War

> **LEARNING SUMMARY**
>
> *After studying this section you will know:*
>
> - how the government recruited for the armed forces, including the use of propaganda, and why people volunteered
> - how the country was organised to fight the war
> - the impact of the war on civilian life
> - the mood of the British people at the end of the war

Recruitment and propaganda

AQA B
OCR B
WJEC A

> At the beginning of the war there was enormous enthusiasm for it – but everyone thought it would be over by Christmas.

Most people in Britain welcomed the start of the war. There was enormous enthusiasm for it. This was because:

- people believed that Britain was fighting for something that was right – defending tiny Belgium against the might of Germany
- many people had romantic ideas of what it would be like, e.g. heroic cavalry charges; nobody thought it would end up with millions being killed
- most people were genuinely patriotic and wanted to fight to defend their country

Britain only had a small full-time army so it was vital to recruit soldiers quickly. At first the enthusiasm for the war made this easy. Men rushed to join: in August 1914 300,000 men joined up. The government played an important part in persuading men to join up:

> Lord Kitchener was Secretary of State for War.

- it encouraged men from the same area or the same factory or business to form '**Pals' battalions**, e.g. 'Glasgow Corporation Tramways', the 'Accrington Pals'
- it also used **propaganda** to put pressure on men to sign up: posters, speeches, newspaper advertisements and leaflets were used

The most famous example is the poster of Kitchener pointing his finger – 'Your country needs you'. Other posters were aimed at women, suggesting that their men were cowards if they would not join up. Some went as far as claiming that men's future children would be ashamed of them. There was even a 'white feather campaign' in which women gave men who had not joined up white feathers as a symbol of their cowardice.

Fig. 1.10 A recruiting poster from 1914.

Propaganda was also used to whip up hatred against the Germans and to maintain morale by giving people a completely misleading impression of what was happening in the trenches. The soldier's life was shown as heroic and glamorous.

Fig. 1.11 A recruiting poster.

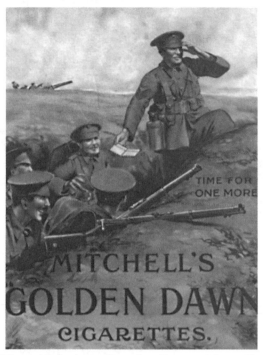

Fig. 1.12 A cigarette advertisement from the First World War.

The large number of men joining the army meant there were fewer left to work in factories and on farms. Women stepped in and did these jobs. For the role of women in the war see pages 19–21.

All these campaigns were so successful that by the end of 1915 2.5 million men had joined the army. However, problems were emerging:

- so many men had been killed on the battlefields that more recruits were needed
- the number of men volunteering was falling

In 1916 the government introduced **conscription.** This meant:

- the government had the power to conscript all men aged 18–41 into the armed forces
- men in essential work, e.g. in munitions factories, were exempt
- conscientious objectors had to justify why they did not want to fight

Organising the country for war

AQA B
OCR B
WJEC A

The *Defence of the Realm Act* (DORA) 1914

In time of war governments often need extra powers to fight effectively. People also often have their rights reduced.

DORA allowed the government to:

- censor the press so it could control how the war was reported in the newspapers – the government wanted people to believe it was going well
- introduce **rationing**

- take any property it needed for the war effort (e.g. factories, land). In 1917 the government ordered an extra 2.5 acres of land to be ploughed for growing food

DORA stopped people:

Why did the government ban these activities?

- talking about military matters in public places
- buying binoculars
- trespassing on railways and bridges
- ringing church bells

Civilian life during the war

AQA B
OCR B
WJEC A

There were civilian casualties in Britain.

- In 1914 towns on the east coast, like Scarborough, were shelled. A total of 119 people were killed.
- Later in the war the Germans sent Zeppelins (airships) to bomb towns in the South-East. Hundreds were killed.

There was a shortage of food.

- At the beginning of the war this was caused by people buying and hoarding large amounts of food.
- Later in the war (1916) the cause was the blockade by German submarines which stopped supply ships getting to Britain.
- Food prices rose steeply and long queues formed at shops. Many poor people could not afford the prices and some suffered from malnutrition.

Some historians argue that the poor had a better diet after rationing was introduced than they had before the war!

- In 1918 the situation was so bad that the government introduced rationing: one pound of meat per head per week; sugar (half a pound), bacon, butter and cheese were also rationed.
- Rationing improved the situation and even the poor were able to have healthy food to eat. Their health had improved by the end of the war.

The mood of the British people at the end of the war

AQA B
OCR B
WJEC A

After four years of fighting, with millions of men dead and after being continuously fed anti-German propaganda during the war, the British public was in the mood for revenge in 1918.

For more about the end of the war and the mood of the victorious countries see pages 40–44.

In the general election of 1918 politicians tried to outdo each other in their demands about how Germany should be punished. The newspapers demanded that the Kaiser be hanged.

Lloyd George, the Prime Minister, was in a difficult position. During the election campaign he said that Germany should be made to pay the whole cost of the war. Later, when he went to the peace negotiations, he realised that punishing Germany too harshly would be a mistake. However, he was constantly under pressure from British public opinion to support a harsh peace treaty.

One member of the government promised that they would 'squeeze the German lemon till the pips squeak'.

Sample GCSE questions

1. Study the following sources.

Source A: A British poster of 1915.

Daddy, what did YOU do in the Great War?

Source B A British poster of 1915.

TO THE
YOUNG WOMEN OF LONDON

Is your "Best Boy" wearing Khaki? If not don't YOU THINK he should be?

If he does not think that you and your country are worth fighting for—do you think he is WORTHY of you?

Don't pity the girl who is alone—her young man is probably a soldier—fighting for her and her country—and for YOU.

If your young man neglects his duty to his King and Country, the time may come when he will NEGLECT YOU.

Think it over—then ask him to

JOIN THE ARMY TO-DAY

Source C

A military band and marching soldiers are always an inspiring sight, but this was for real – they were off to war and how we youngsters envied them. And to tell you the truth that was it – glamour – to be in uniform – and to take part in a great adventure was as much the reason for so many youths joining up as any sense of patriotism.

From a book published some years after the war ended. The author did not join the army until later in the war.

Source D

Many of the older men felt a genuine patriotism. There was a great pride in Britain and the Empire and a general dislike of the Germans. The younger men were almost certainly inspired by the thoughts of adventure and travel at a time when few people had been further than their own city or the nearest seaside resort. The miners, industrial workers and the unemployed often saw the call as a way of escape from their dismal working conditions and overcrowded slums into a new life, where there was fresh air and good companionship, regular meals and all the glamour of the army.

From a history book published in 1971.

Source E

The airship was on fire and it was floating down. I could only think of the people inside it being roasted to death. I was disgusted to see kind, good-hearted British people dancing in the street as the men in that airship were dying. When I said it was a terrible thing, my friends said, 'But they're Germans, they're the enemy, they've been bombing us!' This was what the war did, it turned decent, gentle people into monsters.

A British woman who experienced Zeppelin raids, being interviewed in 1980.

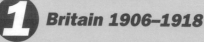

Sample GCSE questions

Source F

Oh, I joined up straight away, August 1914. Ah, what a day that was. Myself and the rest of the fellows leap-frogging down to Cambridge recruiting office and then playing tiddlywinks in the queue. There we were, a crashingly superb bunch of blokes, off to hammer the Boche [Germans].

From the script of a British television comedy programme about the First World War, 1989.

(a) Study Source A. Why was this poster published in Britain in 1915? Use the source and your knowledge to explain your answer. **[6]**

This poster was published in 1915 to persuade men to join the army. The poster shows a father being asked by his children what he did in the war. He looks ashamed because he did not volunteer to fight. This is made worse by the boy playing with toy soldiers and obviously admiring them. The poster is saying that if you do not join up now, much later in life when you have children they will be ashamed of you. They had to publish posters like this because joining the army was still voluntary, and so many men were being killed in the trenches they needed more men all the time.

This answer is a good one because it answers the question by (i) using the source and its details, and (ii) using knowledge of the period. Firstly, the answer explains the message of the poster: this is supported by details from the source. Secondly, the answer uses knowledge to explain why the poster was published in 1915: the references to volunteers and to the numbers of men being killed at the front.

(b) Study Sources A and B. Is one poster more useful than the other to a historian studying Britain during the First World War? Use the sources and your knowledge to explain your answer. **[8]**

I think that Source B is more useful because it shows how pressure was put on young men to join the army. Source B shows how emotional blackmail was used by the government. It says to women that if their man neglects the country then he will probably neglect them as well. This kind of emotional blackmail is similar to women giving men who had not joined up white feathers to show they were cowards. So Source B shows the enormous pressure men were under to join up.

This answer explains the usefulness of Source B very well. The content of the source and knowledge of the period are used to explain how the source demonstrates the pressure that was put on men to join up. The answer is weakened by the fact that Source A has not been used. In questions that ask you to compare the usefulness of two sources, both sources must be analysed.

Sample GCSE questions

(c) Study Sources C and D. How far do these two sources disagree about why men volunteered to join the army? Use the sources to explain your answer. **[6]**

These two sources partly agree and partly disagree about why men volunteered to join the army. They agree because they both say that younger men were attracted by the glamour and the romance of it all. Source C says that they wanted to take part in a great adventure; Source D says the young were inspired by thoughts of adventure. But the sources also differ because Source C suggests this was the only reason people joined up, while Source D says there were other reasons: older men disliked the Germans while other people like miners saw it as a way of getting away from terrible working and living conditions.

This question only requires you to use what is in the sources. There is no need to use any knowledge about the topic. This answer first explains the ways in which the sources agree about why men volunteered, and then explains how they differ. Note how the answer is supported by references to details in the sources.

(d) Study Sources E and F. Is one source more reliable than the other about attitudes in Britain towards the war? Use the source and your knowledge to explain your answer. **[9]**

I think that Source E is reliable because it says that most people hated the Germans during the First World War. It says that they were pleased to see the crew of the airship being burned to death. This is reliable because the government had sent out a lot of propaganda to make people hate the Germans. Stories were spread that the Germans had killed women and children in Belgium. People in Britain attacked shops owned by people with German-sounding names. So this source is reliable about attitudes in Britain.

Source F is also reliable about attitudes. Although it was written for a TV comedy programme and obviously exaggerates to make its point, the basic attitudes it shows were shared by many people at the beginning of the war. Source C shows similar attitudes. Many young men thought it would be a great adventure and joined up as quickly as they could. They thought the war would be over in a few months. They thought it would be fun. Source F is making fun of these attitudes but the attitudes were still there at the beginning of the war. Of course, attitudes changed later in the war when the war dragged on and the casualties grew.

This answer uses knowledge and sources (Source C) from other parts of the question to test the reliability of the two sources. Do not claim that sources are reliable or unreliable simply because they were or were not written at the time, or are by eye-witnesses. Source F is not unreliable simply because it comes from a comedy programme. It may still be reliable about attitudes. You need to examine what the sources actually say. This answer does this and explains how much of what the sources tell us is reliable.

OCR Specimen Paper 2

Chapter

The First World War 1914–1918

The following topics are covered in this chapter:

- The Schlieffen Plan and stalemate
- The other fronts
- The end of the First World War

2.1 The Schlieffen Plan and stalemate

LEARNING SUMMARY

After studying this section you will know:

- why the Schlieffen Plan failed
- what it was like in the trenches
- why the stalemate on the Western Front lasted for so long
- the criticisms and justifications for Haig's tactics in the Battle of the Somme 1916

The failure of the Schlieffen Plan

EDEXCEL A
WJEC A

Germany had long been worried that if a war broke out she would be in danger of having to fight on two fronts: against Russia in the east, and against France in the west. This was because Russia and France, with Britain, belonged to the **Triple Entente**. This was the rival to the **Triple Alliance** to which Germany belonged.

In 1905 Count von Schlieffen had developed the Schlieffen Plan:

- a rapid attack on France through Belgium; Paris to be taken and France defeated within six weeks, before Russia had time to react
- then move the German army to the east to fight Russia

Reasons why the plan did not work

1. On 3 August a German army of over a million men marched into Belgium. The small Belgian army fought very bravely and slowed down the German advance.

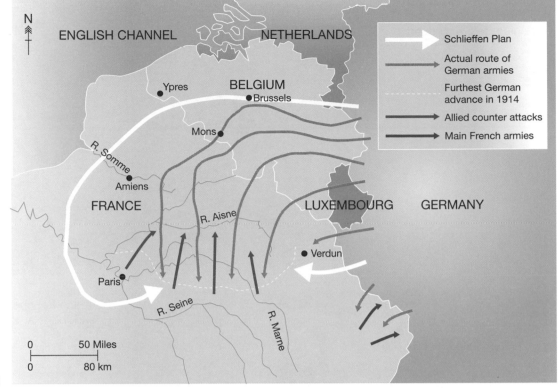

Fig. 2.1

2. Britain had signed the Treaty of London in 1839 promising to protect Belgium. As a result Britain sent the **British Expeditionary Force** to Belgium. The BEF further slowed the Germans at the Battle of Mons.

3. On 19 August Russia invaded Germany (this was much sooner than the Germans had planned for). Germany had to move 100,000 of its troops from the Western to the Eastern Front. This weakened the German advance in the west.

4. The German army continued its advance on Paris but at the Battle of the Marne the British and French armies managed to push the Germans back to the River Aisne where they began to dig trenches. The Schlieffen Plan had failed.

> **KEY POINT** The failure of the Schlieffen Plan was crucial. Its failure dictated the nature of the war for the next four years.

The race to the sea and stalemate

EDEXCEL A
WJEC A

Both sides now raced to get to the English Channel first to outflank each other. At the Battle of Ypres in November, despite thousands of troops being killed, neither side could break through the lines of the other. **Stalemate** had been reached and both sides began to dig trenches to help their defences. By the end of 1914 these trenches stretched from the English Channel to Switzerland.

These trenches stayed almost in the same position until 1918. Major battles were fought but they usually ended with one side or the other gaining no more than a few miles.

Behind the front-line trenches was a system of support trenches used for supplies and reinforcements. They were connected to the front-line trenches by communication trenches.

Fig. 2.2 The Western Front stretched from Belgium to Switzerland

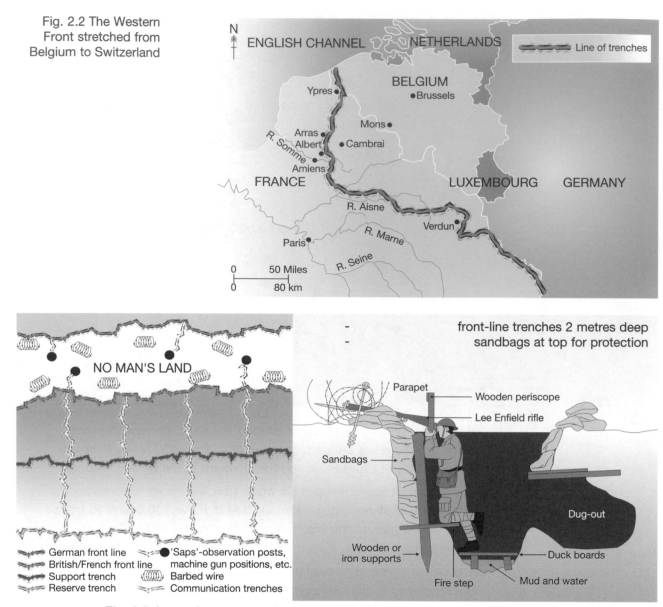

Fig. 2.3 A trench system and a cross-sectional view of a trench.

The area between the British and French trenches, and the German trenches, was called '**No-Man's Land**'. This would often be deep in mud and was covered by line after line of barbed wire to slow down an enemy attack.

The soldiers were meant to spend just a few days at a time in the trenches, but they were sometimes there for weeks, or even months. Life in the trenches was hard and extremely unpleasant. Much of the trench system was built on low-lying land and when it rained the soldiers could be up to their knees in water. This led to many soldiers catching the disorder called trench foot. In winter the trenches were cold, but in summer they were blisteringly hot. Flies and rats were common and the smell from corpses and sewage was terrible. Many soldiers died from disease. Their food – tinned beef and bread or biscuits – was very poor.

For much of the time life in the trenches was boring. A great deal of time was spent on guard duty and repairing the trenches. However, when there was fighting the casualties were terrible. The only way to attack the enemy trenches was by charging across 'No-Man's Land'. In the Battle of the Somme 1.25 million men were killed (57,000 British troops were killed or injured on the first day alone).

Gas

As the war dragged on new weapons were developed by both sides. The most unpleasant of these was gas. The Germans first used chlorine gas in 1915. The wind blew it over the British trenches. Both sides later developed more lethal gases. The most feared was **mustard gas**, which burned, blinded, and even killed. Gas masks were developed to cope with this threat.

Reasons why the stalemate lasted for so long

The stalemate lasted for so long because it was much easier to defend the trenches than to attack them, for the following reasons.

1. The weapons in the First World War were much better for defending than for attacking. As attacking soldiers charged across 'No-Man's Land' they were simply mowed down by machine guns or blown up by land mines. The defenders in the trenches were better protected.

2. 'No-Man's Land' was often deep mud and covered with barbed wire. This made it very difficult for men and horses to charge quickly.

3. Both sides had large reinforcements of men and guns which could easily be brought up to support trenches under attack.

4. The generals were not used to fighting this type of warfare. They could not think of any tactics other than to keep sending men across 'No-Man's Land'.

5. Before an attack the enemy trenches were always bombarded with heavy artillery to 'soften them up'. However, this simply warned the enemy that an attack was coming and took away the element of surprise.

 KEY POINT You will need to be able to explain why a stalemate first developed and why it lasted for so long.

The Battle of the Somme and Field Marshal Haig

In December 1915 **Haig** was appointed as commander of the British forces. He had made his reputation as a cavalry commander on the plains of South Africa. Trench warfare was completely new to him.

In July 1916, Haig launched a major attack on the German lines. The French were only just hanging on at Verdun under a prolonged offensive by the Germans. Haig planned to relieve the pressure on the French.

The German trenches were bombarded for a week before the attack took place. However, the Germans had prepared dug-outs deep under the ground and all the bombardment did was to warn the Germans that a major attack was on its way. The battle lasted from July to November. The losses on both sides were enormous. Haig has been criticised for his tactics in the Battle of the Somme. By the end of the battle the Allies had gained just a few miles of territory. What do you think?

Criticisms of Haig	Arguments in support of Haig
1. Haig could think of no other way of fighting than sending wave after wave of soldiers to their deaths in 'No-Man's Land'. It was soon clear that these attacks were not going to succeed and yet Haig persisted with them. 2. A total of 620,000 British soldiers were killed for just a few miles of territory. Haig had wasted all these lives and the German lines had not been broken. 3. The bombardment had been useless and had just warned the Germans about the attack.	1. The Battle of the Somme did take pressure off Verdun, where the Germans called off their attack. 2. Nobody at that time knew of a different way of fighting so Haig should not be blamed for using these tactics. 3. Haig was trying to bring the war to an end by attacking in the only way he knew.

KEY POINT

Remember – don't be too harsh on Haig. Trench warfare was new to everyone at the time and no one really had any idea about how to cope with it.

2.2 The other fronts

LEARNING SUMMARY

After studying this section you will know:

- *the importance of the war at sea*
- *what happened on the other fronts*

The important thing to consider about these other fronts is whether they had an important effect on the course or the outcome of the war.

The First World War was not restricted to the Western Front. Many people think that the most important of the other fronts was the war at sea, because it was vital for the outcome of the war.

The war at sea

EDEXCEL A
WJEC A

Before the war both Britain and Germany had raced to build as many **'Dreadnought'** battleships as possible. However, there was only one major battle at sea during the First World War. The main importance of the war at sea was:

- to protect ships bringing much needed supplies (especially from the USA), and to keep Allied ports open
- to blockade enemy ports so their supplies were cut off

Achieving these aims was just as important as winning the war on the land.

The Battle of Jutland

This was the only major sea battle. Neither side wanted to risk their expensive battleships. For much of the war the German fleet stayed in port. However, the two fleets met in the Battle of Jutland (in the North Sea) in 1916. The battle was confused and indecisive with the British losing more ships. However, the German fleet retreated to port and stayed there for the rest of the war. Both sides claimed victory.

The blockades

Britain received important supplies, including food, from the USA. The Germans decided to use their submarines (called '**U-boats**') to sink the merchant ships carrying these supplies. During 1915 and 1916 thousands of tons of merchant shipping were sunk. By 1917 Britain only had six weeks' supply of food left. It looked as if the country would be starved into defeat.

However, the U-boat threat was finally defeated by:

> **The war at sea was important for keeping Britain supplied, and for stopping supplies getting through to Germany. You will see later that this was crucial at the end of the war.**

- making merchants ships travel together in **convoys** so they could be protected by warships
- using depth charges to sink the submarines
- using 'Q ships' – these were warships disguised as merchant ships; when submarines surfaced, the 'Q ships' would sink them

British ships successfully blockaded Germany. Germany gradually ran short of food and by 1918 this shortage was one of the factors that made many German people want peace.

The Eastern Front

EDEXCEL A
WJEC A

Remember that Russia attacked Germany in 1914 and ensured that the Schlieffen Plan did not work. The Russian army was enormous (1.3 million men, 3 million by 1917) and was nicknamed 'the steamroller' by the Allies, but it was poorly equipped, badly led and organised. In 1914 it suffered two defeats: at Tannenberg and the Masurian Lakes. Russian losses were enormous. By 1917 more than 2 million Russian soldiers had been killed. The Russians had problems in keeping their army supplied. Time and time again a Russian advance petered out because of lack of supplies.

> **Treaty of Brest-Litovsk 1918: Russia out of the war!**

In March 1918 Russia signed the **Treaty of Brest-Litovsk** with Germany. This brought the war between the two countries to an end and gave Germany a lot of Russian territory. Why did Russia agree to this?

- Tsar Nicholas II took direct command of the armies. This was disastrous and thousands more men were killed.
- The winter of 1916 was very harsh. People in Russia were starving. In 1917 the Tsar was forced to abdicate.
- The new government (the Provisional Government) continued with the war but the situation got worse. Soldiers deserted, others mutinied. By 1917 the army was disintegrating.
- When the Bolsheviks took over in November, the German army was advancing into Russia.
- The Bolshevik Government had little choice but to sign the peace treaty.

The Treaty of Brest-Litovsk meant that Germany now had to fight on only one front, and could move one million men to the Western Front

KEY POINT	The defeat of Russia was a victory for Germany. However, because she was able to move 1 million men to the Western Front, Germany became over-confident and thought she could break through the Allied lines with a large offensive.

The disaster of Gallipoli

EDEXCEL A
WJEC A

You have come across Churchill before. He was one of the 'New Liberals' responsible for the social reforms before the war.

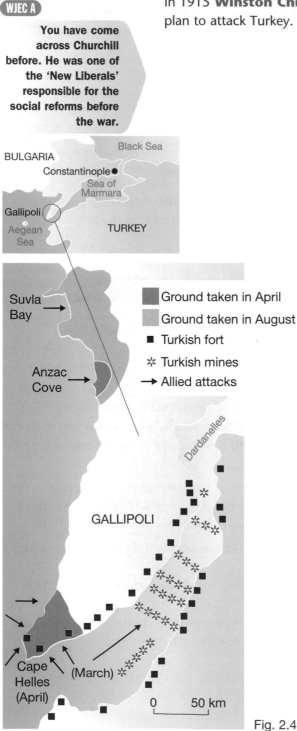

Ground taken in April
Ground taken in August
■ Turkish fort
✳ Turkish mines
→ Allied attacks

Fig. 2.4 The Gallipoli Campaign.

In 1915 **Winston Churchill**, the First Lord of the Admiralty, came up with a plan to attack Turkey.

Why Turkey was attacked

1. Turkey was on Germany's side in the war and was attacking Russia.
2. Britain and France were a long way from Russia and found it difficult to send supplies (remember how short Russia was of supplies). However, supplies could be sent through the Black Sea. The only obstacle to this was Turkey, which controlled **the Dardanelles** – the entrance to the Black Sea.
3. If the Dardanelles could be taken, Turkey could be defeated. This would be a blow to Germany.

The plan

The plan was to take the Gallipoli peninsula – the land to the north of the Dardenelles. This was to be achieved via an attack by the navy, followed by landings on Gallipoli by troops. These were the **ANZACS** – soldiers from Australia and New Zealand.

Reasons why it failed

1. The naval attack went wrong and several battleships were sunk.
2. The naval attack alerted the Turks and when the troops landed they faced heavy fire from Turkish artillery. They were trapped on the beaches and had to dig in. Casualties were high and in December 1915 the navy rescued the surviving troops. A total of 200,000 troops had been killed; 135,000 were rescued.

The war in the air

EDEXCEL A
WJEC A

Airships

In the first years of the war these were more important than planes. Both sides used them.

● The British used airships for escorting merchant ships. They could spot U-boats and warn the warships which were acting as escorts.

● The Germans used their airships (known as **Zeppelins**) to bomb British cities. However, later in the war the Zeppelins were easily dealt with by fighter planes and anti-aircraft guns.

Aeroplanes

At the beginning of the war aeroplanes were extremely basic. They consisted of a wooden frame, canvas, wire and an engine. Crashes were common.

How the uses of aeroplanes changed during the war:

1. First they were used only for reconnaissance. They had no guns and so they just took photographs over enemy trenches. These could give early warnings of enemy attacks or show weak points in enemy positions. They also helped the artillery find the right range for hitting enemy targets.

2. Both sides began to develop fighter aircraft to shoot down the reconnaissance planes. These planes carried machine guns, and as the aircraft became more sophisticated **dogfights** began to develop.

3. By the end of the war the planes were carrying bombs and were able to travel much further so they could even attack cities in enemy countries. By the end of the war the RAF had 23,000 planes (compared to 37 at the beginning of the war).

It is important to remember that the war in the air was nowhere near as important as the war on the land or the war at sea. Aircraft were still too basic to have an important impact on the war.

2.3 The end of the First World War

LEARNING SUMMARY

After studying this section you will know:

● *why the stalemate was broken in 1918*
● *the defeat of Germany*

Breaking of the stalemate and the defeat

EDEXCEL A
WJEC A

On 11 November 1918 Germany signed an **armistice** (ceasefire). Germany had been defeated and the First World War was over. How had the stalemate on the Western Front been broken? There were a number of reasons.

1. One attempt to break the stalemate in the trenches was the development of the tank. It was thought that it would be able to storm across 'No-man's Land' unaffected by enemy machine gun fire. Tanks were first used by the British in the Battle of the Somme but they were slow, some broke down and others got stuck in the mud. As the war went on tanks became more effective and did manage to break through German lines in the Battle of Cambrai in 1917, but only a few miles were gained. In the Battle of Amiens in August 1918 tanks again broke through, starting the Allied offensive which finally led to Germany's defeat. Tanks were not a major factor in breaking the deadlock but they did help.

2. In 1917 the USA entered the war on the side of the Allies because German U-boats had sunk US ships. By 1918 American troops were pouring into France. They were fresh and brought new equipment and supplies with them.

3. By 1918 the German situation was desperate. German ports had been successfully blockaded and both German civilians and soldiers were short of food and raw materials. It was clear that the German army could not go on fighting for very long. A quick victory was needed, especially with more and more American troops arriving in Europe.

4. This led General Ludendorff, the German commander, to launch a last desperate offensive in March 1918. At first the Allies were pushed back and it looked as if the Germans might reach Paris, but by August the German army was exhausted and the attack weakened. The Allies, strengthened by American troops, launched a counter-attack and were soon pushing the German army back.

5. When news of the retreat reached Germany, starving civilians, now being killed in their thousands by influenza, demanded peace. There were riots in the streets.

6. Germany was now isolated. Between September and November 1918, Germany's allies, Bulgaria, Turkey and Austria-Hungary, all surrendered.

Examiner's tip: You need to know the reasons why the stalemate was broken, but more importantly you need to be able to explain these reasons. How did each contribute to the breaking of the stalemate?

PROGRESS CHECK

Below you will find a list of important dates and events. Some are missing. See if you can fill in the gaps.

1. _____ — The Schlieffen Plan is developed
2. 3 August 1914 — _____
3. _____ — The trench system stretches from the English Channel to Switzerland
4. _____ — The disaster of Gallipoli
5. _____ — The Battle of the Somme
6. _____ — The Battle of Jutland
7. 1917 — _____ enters the war
8. March 1918 — _____
9. _____ — Germany signs an armistice.

1. 1905 2. Germany invades Belgium. 3. End of 1914 4. 1915 5. 1916 6. 1916 7. The USA 8. Russia signs the Treaty of Brest-Litovsk. 9. November 1918

Exam practice questions

This question covers topics from both Chapter 1 and Chapter 2, so make sure you have read both chapters.

1. Study Sources A, B, C and D and then answer all parts of the question.

Source A: A crowd in Trafalgar Square, London, at the outbreak of war in 1914

A photograph taken at the time, August 1914

Source B: A recruitment poster

Daddy, what did YOU do in the Great War?

A poster published in Britain in 1914

Source C: A German description from the Battle of the Somme

'Our men at once clambered up the steep shafts leading from the dug-outs and ran for the nearest shell craters. The machine guns were hurriedly put into position. A series of extended lines of British infantry was seen moving forward from the British trenches. They came on at a steady, easy pace as if expecting to find nothing alive in our front trenches.'

From an account by a German soldier of the beginning of the Battle of the Somme in 1916. It was written soon afterwards.

Exam practice questions

Source D: Casualties on the Western Front

After the Battle of the Marne in 1914 the generals had tried to continue the war of manoeuvre. The soldiers, striving gallantly to obey, found that it could not be done. Two new weapons of war – machine guns and barbed wire – prevented movement. The generals said that heavy artillery would be used to blow up the machine guns and destroy the barbed wire. It didn't work. Through 1916 and 1917 despair steadily grew. No one was controlling the war. It was controlling them, with unlimited, endless death.

From Fourteen Eighteen *by John Masters, published in 1965. It consists of articles and photographs that appeared in a British newspaper in the summer of 1964, at the time of the fiftieth anniversary of the outbreak of the First World War.*

(a) What does Source A tell us about how people felt towards the outbreak of war in 1914? **(3)**

....

....

(b) Source B shows a British recruitment poster published in 1914.
Use Source B and your own knowledge to explain why men in Britain volunteered for
the army in 1914.   **(6)**

....

....

....

....

(c) How useful is Source C for explaining why British casualties at the Battle of the Somme
were so high? Use Source C and your own knowledge to answer the question.   **(8)**

....

....

....

....

....

(d) Is Source D a fair interpretation of why there were so many casualties in the First World
War? Use Source D and your own knowledge to answer the question.   **(8)**

....

....

....

AQA Specimen Paper 1

The peace settlements 1919–1923

The following topics are covered in this chapter:

- **The aims of the leading countries**
- **Punishment of the defeated countries**

3.1 The aims of the leading countries

LEARNING SUMMARY

After studying this section you will know:

- **the background to the talks**
- **what the victorious countries wanted to achieve in the peace talks**

The background to the talks

AQA B
OCR B

Germany agreed to a ceasefire on 11 November 1918. The Allies decided to hold a peace conference in Paris in January 1919. The talks were dominated by the '**big three**': **President Wilson of the USA, Prime Minister Lloyd George of Britain**, and **Prime Minister Clemenceau of France**. It is important to remember a number of important points about the background to the talks.

- Germany had to send representatives but their job was simply to accept the terms the Allies agreed. They would not be allowed to take any part in the talks.

- Germany was expecting the peace settlement to be based on President Wilson's idea of 'peace without victory'. The Germans did not accept that they had been defeated in the war and they expected a fair peace settlement.

- The First World War was the most bloody that had ever been fought. Over 8 million soldiers had been killed. The leaders who met in Paris were determined to reach a settlement that would preserve peace for a very long time. The trouble was they also wanted to punish Germany and her allies. Would it be possible to achieve both?

KEY POINT

The peace-makers were trying to achieve two conflicting aims: to punish Germany, and to ensure peace in the future. This made it difficult for them to agree.

France and Georges Clemenceau

Clemenceau wanted Germany to be punished. He had seen his country invaded, large parts of its industry destroyed and millions of its people killed. Clemenceau was determined to make Germany pay compensation to France. He also wanted to weaken Germany so that she could never threaten France again. Clemenceau knew that he had the French people behind him.

Britain and Lloyd George

Examiner's tip: Make sure you can discuss how far the leaders' different aims conflicted and made a settlement difficult to reach.

Lloyd George had been re-elected as Prime Minister 1918 but to win votes he had gone along with the popular mood that Germany should be 'squeezed until the pips squeaked'. However, he really wanted a moderate peace and tried to prevent Germany from being punished too harshly. Whenever he did this he clashed with Clemenceau and was criticised back in Britain. Lloyd George ended up in a mid-way position between the aims of Clemenceau on the one hand, and Wilson on the other.

The USA and Woodrow Wilson

By 'self-determination' Wilson meant each different nation of people having their own country and governing themselves, instead of being ruled by another nationality.

Wilson did not share the anti-German passions of the Europeans. He believed that punishing Germany too harshly would simply make her want revenge and could lead to another war. He wanted a just peace that would last and thought this could be achieved through (i) **self-determination**, and (ii) countries working together in a League of Nations to prevent future war. Wilson's ideas are to be found in his Fourteen Points.

Wilson's Fourteen Points

1. No secret treaties between countries
2. Free access to the sea for all
3. Free trade between countries
4. Disarmament by all countries
5. Colonies to have a say in their own future
6. German troops to leave Russia
7. Belgium to be independent
8. France to regain Alsace-Lorraine
9. Frontier between Austria and Italy to be adjusted
10. Self-determination for people of Eastern Europe
11. Serbia to have access to the sea
12. Self-determination for people in the Turkish Empire
13. Poland to be independent, with access to the sea
14. A League of Nations to settle disputes between countries

Examiner's tip: Be ready to discuss how far Wilson's points were put into practice in the peace treaties.

However, public opinion back in the USA had been affected by the loss of 115,000 US troops who had been killed in the war, and many Americans wanted less involvement in European affairs, not more.

3.2 Punishment of the defeated countries

LEARNING SUMMARY

After studying this section you will understand:

- *the Treaty of Versailles and how Germany reacted*
- *how the other defeated countries were punished*
- *the main issues arising from the peace treaties*

The Treaties

AQA B
OCR B

How Germany was treated: the Treaty of Versailles 1919

Altogether there were five sets of negotiations, each held at a palace around Paris. Each palace gave its name to that part of the peace settlement and to the treaty that resulted. The first treaty to be agreed was the Treaty of Versailles, which dealt with Germany.

The most important parts of the treaty were about punishing Germany and making her weak.

> **Examiner's tip:** You need to be making up your mind now about whether these terms were likely to ensure peace in the future, or whether they would make Germany determined to gain revenge later on.

1. The war-guilt clause	Germany had to accept blame for starting the war.
2. Reparations	Germany had to pay compensation to the Allies for all the damage caused in the war. The amount (set in 1921) was enormous – £6,600 million.
3. The armed forces of Germany	To keep Germany weak her armed forces were strictly limited to the following: the army – 100,000 men (conscription to the army was banned and no German troops were allowed in the Rhineland) equipment – only six battleships, no submarines, planes or tanks
4. Germany's territory	Germany lost land in Europe, particularly Alsace-Lorraine to France and the Saar and Danzig (put under the control of the League of Nations). All Germany's colonies were taken away and put under the control of the League of Nations (the mandates were given to Britain, France and other countries).
5. The League of Nations	The main part of the treaty that was not about Germany was the setting up of the League of Nations. Germany was not allowed to become a member until she had shown herself to be a peaceful country.

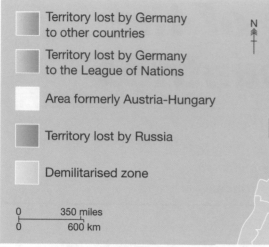

Fig. 3.1 German losses at Versailles.

PEACE AND FUTURE CANNON FODDER

The Tiger: "Curious! I seem to hear a child weeping!"

Fig. 3.2 A British cartoon from 1920 about the Treaty of Versailles. Do you think the cartoonist is supporting or criticising the Treaty?

German reactions to the Treaty of Versailles

The Allies had hoped to make Europe more stable by making Germany weaker. This was not how the Germans saw it. They were very angry. Reasons for their resentment included:

- the treaty was **a diktat**. Germany was threatened with war if she did not accept it.

- the treaty was meant to be based on Wilson's Fourteen Points. One of these was self-determination, but the loss of German lands in Europe meant that many Germans were now being ruled by foreigners, e.g. Germans in the Sudetenland (now part of Czechoslavkia).

- the Germans had been very proud of their army and navy. These were now made powerless. Germans felt humiliated. They were especially angry when it later became clear that countries like Britain and France had no intention of disarming.

- being blamed for starting the First World War. Germans felt this was very unfair because other countries were also involved in the start of the war.

- the effects of reparations, which were crippling. The loss of some of Germany's main industrial areas made it even more difficult for her to pay the reparations. The government tried to solve its problems by issuing more money but this simply led to inflation, which in turn led to massive unemployment. Germany failed to keep up her reparation payments to France who, in 1923, made matters worse by deciding to 'help herself' by invading the Ruhr, Germany's most important industrial area. German workers went on strike in protest. All this disrupted the German economy even more. Inflation worsened, with money becoming worthless. Many Germans blamed all this on reparations and the Treaty of Versailles.

KEY POINT

The German people were angry about the terms of the Treaty of Versailles. They never accepted them and wanted them reversed. Hitler would later be the politician who would promise to do this. See page 59.

Austria: the Treaty of St Germain 1919

1. Austria and Hungary were separated.
2. The new states of Czechoslovakia and Yugoslavia were set up. Austria lost land to both these new countries (this left many Germans in Czechoslovakia).
3. Austria was forbidden to unite with Germany.
4. The size of the Austrian armed forces was limited.

Bulgaria: the Treaty of Neuilly 1919

1. Bulgaria was treated quite leniently but lost some land.
2. The size of the Bulgarian armed forces was limited.

Hungary: the Treaty of Trianon 1920

1. Hungary lost land to Czechoslovakia and Yugoslavia.
2. The size of the Hungarian armed forces was limited.

Turkey: the Treaty of Sèvres 1920

1. Turkey lost land to Greece. It also lost Palestine, Iraq, Transjordan and Syria which were put under the control of the League of Nations (Britain and France were given the mandates).

Important issues about the peace settlements

More information about the League of Nations can be found in Chapter 4.

- The treaties were harsh on the defeated countries, especially Germany. Would this help to keep the peace in future or would it lead to trouble?
- Germany was left feeling humiliated. The German economy was in desperate trouble. All this would lead to problems in the future.
- Self-determination had not really been achieved. There were 2 million Germans living in Czechoslovakia – this would lead to future trouble. In fact, countries like Czechoslovakia and Poland had many different nationalities living within their borders.
- Germany, Russia and the USA were all missing from the League of Nations. Would this make it powerless?
- It is easy to criticise the treaties now but was it possible to do any better at the time?

PROGRESS CHECK

Below you will find a list of some of the defeated countries and some of the terms of the peace treaties. See if you can fill in the gaps.

Country	Terms
1. Germany	Had to pay reparations of _____
2.	Newly formed countries _____
3. Austria	Not allowed to unite with _____
4. _____	Blamed for causing the First World War
5. _____	Lost land to Czechoslovakia and Yugoslavia
6. _____	Lost Alsace-Lorraine, the Saar and Danzig
7. Turkey	Lost _____
8. Germany	Armed forces reduced to _____

1. £6,600 million 2. Czechoslovakia and Yugoslavia 3. Germany 4. Germany 5. Austria 6. Germany 7. land to Greece, Palestine, Iraq, Transjordan and Syria. 8. 100,000 men

Sample GCSE questions

1. **Source A**

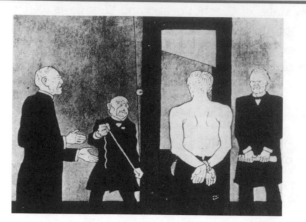

A German cartoon about the Treaty of Versailles. Clemenceau prepares to guillotine a figure representing Germany as Wilson and Lloyd George look on.

(a) Study Source A. What is the cartoonist suggesting about the Treaty of Versailles? Explain your answer, referring to details of the cartoon. **[6]**

The cartoonist is suggesting that the Treaty of Versailles is too harsh and will do great damage to Germany. This is shown by the fact that Germany is going to be executed. The cartoonist is saying that terms such as making Germany pay huge reparations and lose her main industrial areas like the Saar would ruin Germany. The cartoonist is also showing that Clemenceau is much keener on being harsh to Germany than Wilson or Lloyd George. This is why Clemenceau is pulling the rope for the guillotine and the others seem to look unhappy about it. Clemenceau wanted to get revenge on Germany for all the suffering France had endured in the First World War.

(b) In what ways was President Wilson dissatisfied with the Treaty of Versailles? Explain your answer. **[9]**

Wilson was dissatisfied with the Treaty of Versailles for several reasons. He had hoped that the peace treaty would be based on his Fourteen Points and that it would not punish Germany too harshly. He thought that if Germany was punished harshly she would want revenge and this would make it harder to keep international peace. But Germany was very harshly punished and he was unhappy about this. He did not support the enormous reparations Germany had to pay and thought it was unwise to take too much land away from Germany. He was also disappointed that self-determination was not achieved everywhere. He wanted different nationalities to be able to govern themselves but the new countries like Czechoslovakia and Yugoslavia had lots of different nationalities within their boundaries, including Germans. This meant they did not have self-determination.

OCR Paper 1, 1998

With source questions like this you must make sure you:

(i) say what the message of the cartoonist is

(ii) support this by using the details in the cartoon

(iii) and support this by using your knowledge – but make sure you only use your knowledge to support a point you are making about the cartoon. Do not just write everything you know about the Treaty of Versailles.

Make sure you give more than one reason (two will be fine). This answer explains two reasons.

Give specific examples of aspects of the treaty that Wilson was unhappy about. Avoid making general points.

Once you have given a specific example, make sure you **explain** why Wilson was unhappy with it.

The League of Nations

The following topics are covered in this chapter:

- The setting up of the League
- The League in action in the 1920s
- Failures of the League in the 1930s

4.1 The setting up of the League

LEARNING SUMMARY

After studying this section you will know:

- the part played by Woodrow Wilson in setting up the League
- the aims of the League
- how the League was organised
- which important countries were members of the League, and which were not
- the League's strengths and weaknesses

The role of Woodrow Wilson

AQA B
OCR B

In January 1920 the Council of the League of Nations met for the first time. This was largely due to the ideas and efforts of Woodrow Wilson, the US President.

More information about Wilson's Fourteen Points can be found on page 41.

Before the First World War it was thought that the balance-of-power system would preserve peace. The blood and gore of this war (nearly 10 million soldiers died) showed that a new system was needed. Wilson genuinely hated war. He had supported America's entry into the war in 1917 only because he thought this would give the US influence to bring about a war-less world. Wilson was important to the setting up of the League because:

Collective security meant that if peace was threatened, all the other countries would unite against the aggressor.

- he suggested setting up a League of Nations in his famous Fourteen Points speech of 1918
- he made sure the League was included in the peace treaties
- it was his idea that the League would replace the balance-of-power system with a system based on collective security

The aims of the League

AQA B
OCR B

To be able to make an assessment about how successful the League was you first need to understand its aims. These were stated in its Covenant, and were:

- to achieve international peace

Examiner's tip:
You need to know these aims and be ready to assess how far the League fulfilled them.

- to encourage nations not to resort to war when in dispute with each other, but to settle their disputes peacefully
- if necessary, to take action against aggressors
- to reduce the armaments held by each state
- to improve working conditions of people around the world
- to encourage nations to co-operate in areas like fighting disease and slavery

The organisation of the League

AQA B
OCR B

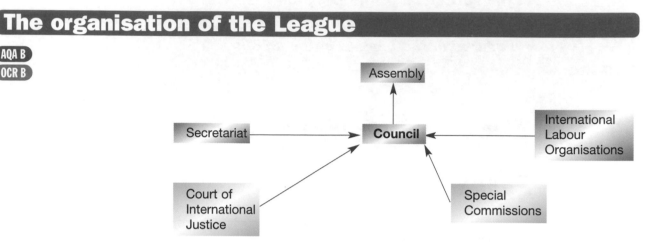

Fig. 4.1 Organisation of the League of Nations.

The Covenant also set out how the League was to be organised.

The Assembly

This was where all the representatives from each member country met.

- Each country had one vote.
- The Assembly could discuss and decide on any matter, but it usually only met once a year.
- Decisions had to be unanimous.

The Assembly was too big, and did not meet often enough to deal with crises as they occurred and so a Council was also set up.

The Council

There were four permanent members: Britain, France, Italy and Japan (five in 1926 when Germany was admitted).

Did the League's organisation help or hinder it?

- There were four temporary members (increased later, e.g. to six in 1922). They were elected by the Assembly.
- It met at least four times a year.
- Permanent members had a **veto**, i.e. they could stop the Council from making a decision.

The Assembly and the Council needed help with their work and so a Secretariat was set up.

The Secretariat

This was the civil service of the League. It got papers ready for meetings, kept records of meetings and prepared reports. It was based at Geneva in Switzerland.

Two important bodies set up by the League were the Court of International Justice and the International Labour Organisation.

The Court of International Justice

This was based at The Hague in Holland. Its judges were from different countries and it decided on disputes between member countries. It had no way of enforcing its decisions but it did settle over 70 major cases in the 1920s and 1930s.

The International Labour Organisation

Examiner's tip: Make sure you know one or two examples of the League's work in these areas.

Its aim was to improve working conditions. Each country sent representatives to its annual meeting. Workers and employers were represented as well as governments. It collected information about working conditions and made suggestions to improve conditions.

Special Commissions

These were set up for specific problems. Examples include drugs, slavery, health and mandated territories.

Membership of the League

The League started with 42 members and by the 1930s there were nearly 60. However, three important countries were not members at first.

Fig. 4.2 A British cartoon commenting on American absence from the League.

- The USA. Many Americans wanted to stay out of European affairs. They thought Europe would involve them in wars and Americans would be killed. They also thought that America would end up paying for much of the work of the League. America never joined the League.
- Germany was not allowed to join the League. Many countries still did not trust Germany. Germany would be allowed in once it had proved itself to be a responsible country. Germany joined in 1926.
- The USSR. Russia became communist in 1917. The Russians regarded the League as a club of capitalist countries who were the enemies of communism. The other great powers were also suspicious of Russia and afraid of communism. But Russia joined in 1934.

 KEY POINT Some of the 'ins' and 'outs' of the League. Britain and France in all the time. The USA out all the time. Germany in 1926, out 1933. The USSR in 1934, out 1939. Japan in 1920, out 1933.

The powers of the League

AQA B
OCR B

> Were these powers likely to be strong enough?

To be effective the League needed to be able to enforce its decisions. However, its powers were rather weak, and not very clear.

- If a member of the League attacked another country, or ignored a decision made by the League, the League could impose economic sanctions.
- If economic sanctions did not work, the member countries of the League would put together armed forces to enforce its decisions.

The League's weaknesses and strengths

AQA B
OCR B

> Examiner's tip: Remember to use specific examples to explain these reasons. You need to look at the sections on the League in action to find these examples, pages 50–53.

Weaknesses	Strengths
• The United States, the most powerful country in the world, did not join. Many Americans wanted to stay out of European quarrels. • Other powerful countries like Germany and the USSR were not members at first. The League depended on Britain and France but neither was as powerful as it used to be. • The League depended on member countries putting their own interests second to what was best for everyone. Not many countries were willing to do this. • Decisions in the Assembly and the Council had to be unanimous. This might make it difficult for the League to come to decisions and act. • Economic sanctions were difficult to enforce because they often harmed the countries imposing the sanctions. • The League had no armed forces with which to enforce its decisions. It had little chance of raising an army without powerful countries like the USA as members. Britain and France could not afford to supply all the troops. Countries like Germany did not like the peace settlement and one day would challenge it.	• A total of 42 countries did join (and more joined later). • The aims of the League were widely supported and the members did genuinely want to co-operate and avoid another war. • The League could impose damaging economic sanctions on aggressive nations.

1. Write down five words that summarise the aims of the League.
2. Describe the organisation of the League.
3. Name four strengths and four weaknesses of the League.

PROGRESS CHECK

1. Peace, co-operation, disarmament, discussion, anti-slavery. 2. The League was organised into an Assembly where all the members met, a Council which made the decisions, and a Secretariat which did all the paper work. 3. Strengths: 42 countries joined, could impose economic sanctions, most countries did not want another war, aims of the League had wide support; Weaknesses: USA did not join, it had no army, decisions had to be unanimous, economic sanctions were hard to enforce.

4.2 The League in action in the 1920s

LEARNING SUMMARY

After studying this section you will know:

- **some examples of its work in trying to settle disputes in the 1920s**
- **some examples of its work in economic and social areas**
- **about attempts at disarmament and the other main international agreements of the 1920s**
- **how the League reacted to the Manchurian and Abyssinian crises**

Now you know about the organisation of the League and its weaknesses and strengths, have a look at what happened when the League had to deal with disputes between countries. In this section we are going to concentrate on the 1920s.

The League and political problems

AQA B
OCR B

The League was involved in many disputes in the 1920s. Here are some case studies of a few of these disputes. You will not need to know about others. For each case study try and decide whether the League was (i) successful, (ii) a failure, or (iii) somewhere in between the two.

> The Conference of Ambassadors included representatives from Britain, France, Italy and Japan. Its job was to deal with matters arising from the peace settlement, but it was sometimes used in place of the League.

(i) Vilna 1920–1923

The city of Vilna was given to Poland in the peace settlement. Most of the people living there were Jews and Poles. However, Lithuania claimed the city. In 1920 the Russians occupied Vilna and handed it over to their ally Lithuania. Poland appealed to the League, which appointed a Commission. However, a Polish army then attacked Vilna. The League suggested a plebiscite but no settlement was reached. In 1923 the Conference of Ambassadors awarded Vilna to Poland without consulting the League.

A success or a failure?

(ii) The Aaland Islands 1920–1921

These islands are near Finland but the language and culture of the people was Swedish. When Finland gained its independence from Russia in 1917 the islanders declared their loyalty to Sweden. The Finns sent troops to the islands. The dispute was taken to the League in 1920, which set up a Commission of Enquiry. In 1921 the Commission recommended a compromise – the islands should remain formally under Finnish authority but with guarantees protecting their Swedish language and culture. Both sides accepted.

A success or a failure?

(iii) Corfu 1923

In 1923 an Italian general was shot dead while working on a boundary dispute between Greece and Albania (Italy's ally). Mussolini claimed compensation from Greece within 24 hours and then bombarded and invaded the island of Corfu, which belonged to Greece.

The Greeks appealed to the League and to the Conference of Ambassadors. Mussolini claimed the League had no right to intervene and said the issue should be decided by the Conference of Ambassadors. He even threatened to leave the League. The League handed the whole matter over to the Conference of Ambassadors which ordered Mussolini to leave Corfu, but also made Greece pay Italy compensation.

A success or a failure?

(iv) The French invasion of the Ruhr 1923

France accused Germany of not keeping up with reparation payments. French and Belgian troops occupied the industrial Ruhr region of Germany. France planned to take German coal and steel but the German workers went on strike.

A success or a failure?

(v) Greece and Bulgaria 1925

In October 1925 a border clash between Greek and Bulgarian troops led to Greek troops advancing into Bulgaria. The League acted decisively and by the end of October the fighting had stopped and Greece had agreed to withdraw her troops. The League then set up a Commission of Enquiry which made Greece pay compensation to Bulgaria.

A success or a failure?

> It is often claimed that the League was successful in disputes involving minor countries, but when the major powers were involved the League was powerless. Do you agree?

The League's other work

It can be argued that the most important work of the League was social and economic rather than political. Here are some examples of what it achieved.

Refugees

At the end of the war there were 3 million refugees who had fled from their homelands. They had no homes, food or jobs. The League gave them passports, which helped them settle in new countries. The League also returned about 400,000 prisoners to their homes.

Health

> Examiner's tip: Don't forget the economic and social work of the League when making an assessment of its success.

The Health Organisation of the League was effective. It organised educational campaigns, distributed medicines, trained health officers and set up clinics for children. It started a worldwide campaign to exterminate mosquitoes which helped reduce cases of malaria. In the 1930s it virtually took over and ran the public health system in China. However, it had little success trying to stop the international drug trade.

Slavery

The League persuaded member countries to recognise that slavery and the slave trade were wrong. It did not end slavery worldwide but had some successes, e.g. 200,000 slaves were freed in Sierra Leone.

Women and children

The League had some success in reducing the trade of women for sexual purposes and in protecting children from abuse.

The International Labour Organisation

This was probably the most successful of the League's agencies. It got member countries to agree to:

- a reduction in working hours
- the right of workers to join a trade union
- a minimum working age of 15

However, not all member countries enforced these measures.

Fig. 4.3 Cartoon about disarmament.

Disarmament

One of the aims of the League was to reduce armaments. However, in the years immediately after the war countries like the USA and Britain increased spending on their navies.

At the Washington Conference of 1921–1922 the main powers, including the USA, agreed to reduce the size of their navies. There were other attempts at disarmament in the 1920s but they all failed.

Other international agreements

Despite the failure of the League to reduce armaments, some progress was made in creating a more peaceful world. This was achieved through a series of international agreements.

The most important were the Locarno Treaties and the Kellogg–Briand Pact.

The Locarno Treaties 1925

These agreements brought Germany back into the international community and paved the way for Germany's admittance into the League in 1926. They seemed to represent a new era of co-operation.

- Germany accepted the borders with France and Belgium as laid down in the Treaty of Versailles.
- Britain and Italy guaranteed to protect these borders if Germany threatened them.
- Germany accepted that the Rhineland should remain demilitarised.
- France agreed to withdraw all troops from the Ruhr.
- France and Germany agreed to take all disputes to the League.

Did the fact that these agreements were made outside the League reduce its importance?

The Kellogg–Briand Pact 1928

This was signed by 15 countries, including the USA, which all agreed that they would not use war to settle disputes with other countries. Like Locarno, this agreement promised a peaceful world.

PROGRESS CHECK

1. Name two successes and two failures of the League in dealing with disputes between countries.
2. Briefly explain why the League failed in dealing with some disputes but succeeded with others.
3. Name three achievements of the League in social matters.
4. Briefly explain why by 1928 many people were optimistic about international peace.

1. Successes: the Aaland Islands, Greece and Bulgaria. Failures: Vilna, the Ruhr. 2. Reasons include: the League could deal with disputes involving minor powers, but could not stand up to powerful countries. 3. Improving working conditions; reduction in child labour; slavery abolished in some parts of the world. 4. This was because of the Locarno Treaties and the Kellogg–Briand Pact.

4.3 Failures of the League in the 1930s

LEARNING SUMMARY

After studying this section you will know:

● **why the 1930s was a difficult period in which to try and keep the peace**
● **why the League failed in the crisis over Manchuria**
● **why the League failed in the crisis over Abyssinia**

In the 1930s the world became a much more difficult place for the League to deal with. This was because of:

● the Great Depression
● its failure to reach any agreement about disarmament
● aggressive policies by Japan in Manchuria, and by Italy in Abyssinia
● the aggressive policies of Hitler's Germany (we will be looking at this in the next chapter)

The effects of the Great Depression

AQA B
OCR B

For the Wall Street Crash see page 58.

Examiner's tip:
Make sure you know two or three specific examples of why it was more difficult to get countries to co-operate in the 1930s than in the 1920s.

In 1929 the Wall Street Crash in the USA sparked off an economic depression throughout the world. Millions of people were thrown out of work. This made the League's work harder in the following ways.

● Trade between countries declined and this led to countries like the USA putting tariffs on imports from outside to protect their own industries and jobs. This, in turn, damaged relations between these countries.
● Some countries like Britain did not want to get involved in settling international disputes while they had economic problems like high unemployment.
● In Germany the economic depression led to Hitler being elected to power. He promised to overthrow the Treaty of Versailles and take back by force the land Germany had lost at Versailles. This led to France's refusal to disarm and she started building up her defences.

For the Manchurian Crisis see below.

For the Abyssinian Crisis see below.

- To rescue its industry from collapse Japan invaded and conquered Manchuria.
- To distract the Italian people's attention away from Italy's economic problems Mussolini invaded Abyssinia.

Disarmament

AQA B
OCR B

World Disarmament Conference, Geneva 1932–33

A total of 59 countries were present but the conference collapsed without any agreement. Germany wanted other countries to disarm; France did not want to reduce its armed forces because of its fear of being attacked again. In 1933 Germany withdrew from the conference. Everyone knew that Hitler was rearming Germany and so the conference collapsed with no agreement.

Two crises for the League

AQA B
OCR B

In the 1930s the League faced two major crises. Its future depended on how well it dealt with these crises.

Fig. 4.4 Map of the Manchurian crisis.

Crisis No. 1: the Japanese invasion of Manchuria 1931

In 1931 Japan invaded Manchuria (part of China). Why?

- The economic depression hit Japan very hard because it depended so much on trading with other countries. Trade with the USA and other countries slumped so the Japanese turned their attention to Manchuria. They already controlled the railway there and Manchuria had rich natural resources like coal and iron. It would also provide Japan with a market for its goods and living space for Japan's fast-growing population.
- The military in Japan were keen for Japan to expand and become a powerful nation.

The crisis was sparked off by a bomb which blew up part of the railway near Mukden in September 1931. Japan blamed China but the Japanese may have planted the bomb to give them an excuse to invade.

Examiner's tip:
Can you find examples of the following factors which caused the League to fail?

- **The absence of the USA**
- **Britain not keen on doing anything**
- **The need for the League's decisions to be unanimous**
- **The slowness of the League in doing anything**

How are these crises different to the earlier crises in the 1920s where the League succeeded?

This is what then happened.

September 1931	China appealed to the League for help. The League asked the USA to be involved in a Commission of Enquiry. The USA did not want to get involved. Britain had few economic interests in Manchuria and so was not that interested in what happened there. The League asked both sides to resume normal relations and did not even impose economic sanctions on Japan.
October 1931	Japan vetoed a Council resolution calling for the withdrawal of Japanese forces.
November 1931	The League set up a Commission of Enquiry under Lord Lytton. Japan, meanwhile, knowing that the European powers would not support any action against her, continued the conquest of Manchuria.
September 1932	The Lytton Commission finally reported. It condemned the Japanese invasion.
March 1933	Japan left the League and kept control of Manchuria. The League had failed!

Crisis No. 2: the Italian invasion of Abyssinia in 1935

In 1935 Italy invaded Abyssinia (now called Ethiopia). Why?

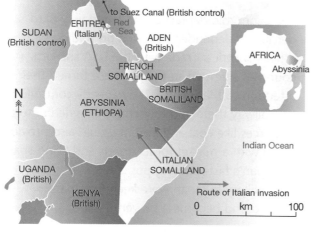

Fig. 4.5 Map of the Abyssinian crisis.

- Mussolini, Italy's Fascist dictator, wanted something to distract the Italian people's attention away from the country's desperate economic problems. A 'foreign adventure' would do this.
- Italy already had the colonies of Eritrea and Somaliland in this part of Africa. Abyssinia would fit in with these very well.
- Abyssinia had resources like coal and oil, whereas Italy's other African possessions amounted to 'a worthless collection of deserts'.
- In 1896 the Abyssinians had defeated Italy at the Battle of Adowa – Mussolini wanted revenge.
- Mussolini wanted to rebuild the glory of the ancient Roman Empire.
- Mussolini had just seen Japan get away with invading Manchuria. Why shouldn't he do the same thing in Abyssinia?

KEY POINT

Mussolini's real reasons for wanting Abyssinia were very different from the reasons he gave at the time (see page 56).

The crisis was sparked off by a border incident between Abyssinian and Italian troops at the end of 1934. Mussolini used this as an excuse to claim land in Abyssinia. He also claimed that it was 'Italy's mission to civilise the black continent' – a reference to the fact that slavery still existed in Abyssinia. The League of Nations was, of course, trying to eliminate slavery.

This is what then happened.

Examiner's tip:
Can you find examples of the following factors which caused the League to fail?

- **The USA and other countries were not members of the League**
- **Britain and France put their own interests first**
- **The League had no army**

January 1935	Haile Selassie, the Emperor of Abyssinia, asked the League to intervene because of the threats Italy was making. The League dithered.
March 1935	Hitler announced he was expanding the German army. Italy, France and Britain met at Stresa. They formed the 'Stresa Front' and condemned what Hitler was doing. Britain and France wanted to keep Italy on their side. They certainly didn't want to drive Italy into Germany's arms! Mussolini may have got the impression they wouldn't act if he invaded.
October 1935	A strong and well equipped Italian army invaded Abyssinia.
October 1935	The League imposed economic sanctions on Italy but oil was not included in these sanctions. Countries who were not members of the League, like the USA, still traded with Italy.
December 1935	The Foreign Ministers of Britain and France, Hoare and Laval, drew up a plan which virtually gave Abyssinia to Italy.
December 1935	The plan was leaked and there was a public outcry against this betrayal of Abyssinia.
March 1936	The League debated whether to add oil to the sanctions but Britain and France were not keen, especially since Germany had just reoccupied the Rhineland.
May 1936	The Italian army completed its conquest of Abyssinia. Its army was much better equipped than the Abyssinian army.
June 1936	It was clear the League had failed.

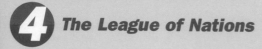

Exam practice questions

1.

(a) What were the main aims of the League of Nations? **(4)**

....

....

....

....

....

(b) Explain why some major nations were not members of the League when it was first set up? **(6)**

....

....

....

....

....

....

....

(c) 'The most important reason why the League was weak in the 1920s was its lack of an army.' Do you agree with this statement? Explain your answer. **(10)**

....

....

....

....

....

....

....

....

....

....

5 Hitler's foreign policy 1933–1939

The following topics are covered in this chapter:

- *The political effects of the Great Depression*
- *Hitler's foreign policy aims*
- *The five steps to war*

5.1 The Great Depression

LEARNING SUMMARY

After studying this section you will know:
- *how the Wall Street Crash led to the Great Depression*
- *how the Great Depression affected countries across the world*

Political effects of the Depression

AQA B
OCR B

For more details about the Wall Street Crash see Chapter 13.

In 1929 the Wall Street Crash in America led to an economic depression. You will need to know how this led to the Great Depression across the world, and what the political effects of the Depression were.

> In 1929 the value of shares on Wall Street in America suddenly plunged. People who had owned shares were ruined. Banks and companies went bankrupt and many people became unemployed.

> The Depression spread to other countries because America stopped buying goods from other countries. This led to unemployment in these countries.

Protectionism is when a country charges high duties on goods from other countries. This makes these goods more expensive than the same goods being made within that country. This leads to people not buying foreign goods.

> It was all made worse when America stopped lending money to other countries

> Some countries introduced protectionism. This made the Depression worse by slowing down world trade.

> The unemployment, poverty and homelessness which resulted then had political consequences. In several countries people turned to right-wing extremism.

For more detail about Hitler and his rule in Germany see pages 147–160.

> In Germany people lost confidence in the government and supported Hitler who came to power in 1933. He promised full employment. He also promised to overturn the terms of the Treaty of Versailles and to make Germany great again.

For more detail about the Italian invasion of Abyssinia see pages 55–56.

You have already seen that the Fascist leader in Italy, Mussolini, launched the invasion of Abyssinia in 1935 to distract Italians from the economic problems in Italy.

↓

For more detail about the Japanese invasion of Manchuria see pages 54–55.

Japan was hit hard by the Depression. Her most important export was silk which was a luxury item that other countries, including America, simply stopped buying. The army leaders became more and more powerful and, as you have seen, launched the invasion of Manchuria in 1931. They thought this would help Japan with its economic problems because it provided raw materials for Japan and living space for its population.

↓

The Depression also had the effect of making America concentrate on her own domestic problems and she took little interest in what was happening in the rest of the world.

PROGRESS CHECK

1. Explain how the Wall Street Crash in America led to economic depression in other countries.
2. Explain what protectionism means.
3. Give three examples of the Depression leading to countries adopting aggressive foreign policies.

1. America stopped buying goods from other countries. This put people out of work. It was made worse when other countries introduced protectionism. This slowed down world trade and everybody suffered from this with more unemployment following. 2. Protectionism refers to countries trying to protect their own industries and jobs. They put heavy import duties on goods coming from other countries. This makes imported goods more expensive and so the goods made at home can be cheaper and sell more. 3. Mussolini's invasion of Abyssinia, Japan's invasion of Manchuria, Germany under Hitler.

5.2 Hitler's foreign policy aims

LEARNING SUMMARY

After studying this section you will know:

- *Hitler's first acts and aims*
- *the results of Hitler's growth in confidence*

Hitler comes to power

AQA B
OCR B
NICCEA

For more detail on the Disarmament Conference see page 54.

Because of the Depression the world was becoming a more dangerous place, but the real turning point was in 1933 when Hitler came to power in Germany. His first acts were not encouraging.

- He walked out of the Disarmament Conference in 1933. He did not see why the size of Germany's armed forces should remain restricted by the Treaty of Versailles while other countries did little about disarmament.

● he also took Germany out of the League of Nations. The League's job was to defend the Treaty of Versailles. Hitler was determined to destroy it.

Hitler's foreign policy was influenced by his ideas about race, which he described in ***Mein Kampf*** in 1924, while in prison. He believed the **Aryan** races were superior to all other races, and the Germans the most superior of the Aryan races. He believed the most inferior races included the Jews and the Slavs.

This led to the following aims:

Lebensraum means 'living space'. For Hitler it meant conquering land in the east for colonisation. He thought Germany was over-populated, and needed more land to guarantee future food supplies. Note that the Japanese also invaded Manchuria in 1931 for 'living space'.

● to make Germany great again. This would involve ignoring the terms of the Treaty of Versailles, rearming, and taking back land Germany had lost in the Treaty.
● rearmament – Hitler was determined to build up Germany's armed forces. This was not allowed by Versailles.
● to recover the lands Germany had lost in the Treaty of Versailles and to build a **Greater Germany** where all the German people could live together
● to expand into Eastern Europe and Russia, which would provide **Lebensraum** or living space for the growing German population. He justified this by the fact that these areas were inhabited by the races he believed were inferior – Jews and Slavs.

KEY POINT You can see from these aims that Hitler did not make a secret of what his aims were. Remember this when you later read about what he did and how other countries let him get away with it.

Hitler grows in confidence

AQA B
OCR B
NICCEA

Hitler no doubt took notice of the fact that both Japan (in Manchuria in 1931) and Italy (in Abyssinia in 1935) had got away with aggression. He was also encouraged by the plebiscite which had taken place in **the Saar** in January 1935. The Saar had been taken away from Germany by the Treaty of Versailles and administered by the League of Nations. It was an important industrial area and had large coal deposits. In the plebiscite, 90 per cent of the people living there voted to rejoin Germany. This had been allowed for under the Treaty of Versailles and was carried out just seven weeks later.

Hitler now felt confident enough to announce his programme of rearmament for Germany. When he came to power Germany's military position was extremely weak. Hitler simply ignored the terms of the Treaty of Versailles and began to build up the German army. In 1935 he introduced conscription and began to build a German air force and a navy. Britain and France did little about this, and in 1935 Britain even signed a **Naval Agreement** with Germany which allowed Germany's navy to be 35 per cent of the size of the British navy. This agreement broke the Treaty of Versailles and is the first example of Britain practising the policy of **appeasement** towards Germany. France was furious.

KEY POINT

There is agreement about what Hitler's aims were but historians disagree about how he planned to achieve them. Some argue that he had a plan from the beginning which he followed step by step; others argue that he simply acted when opportunities were right.

PROGRESS CHECK

1. Name four of Hitler's foreign policy aims.
2. Explain what Hitler meant by the 'Aryan' race.
3. How did the plebiscite result in the Saar and the Naval Agreement with Britain encourage Hitler to become more aggressive?

1. Make Germany a great country; reclaiming land lost at Versailles; expand into Eastern Europe and Russia; build a Germany where all German people could live together. 2. Hitler believed the Ayran race was the most superior race. Germans were the most superior of the Ayran races. 3. The plebiscite result in the Saar encouraged Hitler to be more aggressive because it showed that the people there wanted to be part of Germany. This encouraged him in his idea of a 'Greater Germany'. The Naval Agreement broke the Treaty of Versailles and allowed Germany to expand its navy. This fitted in with Hitler's rearmament plans.

5.3 The five steps to war

LEARNING SUMMARY

After studying this section you will know:

- ***the five steps to war***
- ***the role of appeasement***

Hitler makes his first moves

AQA B
OCR B
NICCEA

By 1936, with German rearmament under way and with the other major powers distracted by the Italian invasion of Abyssinia, Hitler decided it was time to make his first move.

Step 1 Germany sends troops into the Rhineland 1936

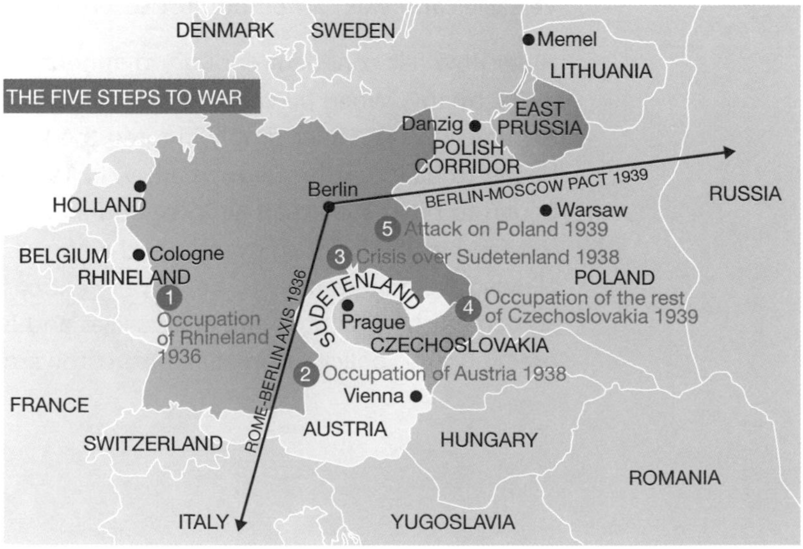

Fig. 5.1 The five steps to war.

Fig. 5.2
A British
cartoon about
the occupation
of the
Rhineland
in 1936.

THE GOOSE-STEP.

The Rhineland had been turned into a demilitarised zone by the Treaty of Versailles. This was because it was part of Germany on the border with France. It was thought that keeping German troops out would help protect France from invasion. In March 1936 Hitler ordered German troops into the Rhineland. The German army was not yet ready to fight a major war and it might seem that Hitler was taking a big risk. He was breaking the terms of the Treaty of Versailles, but he had chosen his time very carefully.

- Remember – the League of Nations and the major powers were all busy dealing with the Italian invasion of Abyssinia.

> You will become familiar with this pattern – Hitler acts aggressively and other countries either ignore what he does or claim that he is justified in what he is doing.

- Hitler also gambled on the fact that Britain would not take action. Many people in Britain felt that Germany should be allowed to have troops in the Rhineland, especially since the USSR and France had just signed a Mutual Assistance Treaty and Hitler claimed Germany was surrounded.
- France was facing a general election and therefore had other things to worry about.

The League of Nations protested, Britain and France protested, but no one actually did anything about it. Hitler later claimed:

'The 48 hours after the march into the Rhineland in 1936 were the most nerve-racking of my life. If the French had opposed us then we would have had to withdraw. Our forces were not strong enough even to put up a moderate resistance.'

This has led some historians to claim that Britain and France could have stopped Hitler in 1936 if they had stood up to him. The policy of appeasement was now well under way.

Step 2

The Anschluss with Austria 1938

Remember, one of Hitler's aims was to build a Greater Germany with all Germans living in it. It was natural for him to make his first move to achieve this aim with Austria. He was born in Austria, and he knew many Austrians regarded themselves as Germans and wanted to be unified with Germany. Such a union, however, was forbidden by the Treaty of Versailles.

By now Hitler was feeling much more confident:

- his army was much larger
- the League of Nations had been shown to be ineffective
- Germany had signed **the Anti-Comintern Pacts** with Japan and Italy, opposing communism
- the British Government gave Hitler the impression it would not oppose Austria and Germany joining together

How did Hitler achieve the Anschluss?

1. In February 1938, Hitler complained to Schuschnigg, the Austrian Chancellor, that Austrian Nazis were being mistreated.

2. Hitler forced Schuschnigg to accept two Austrian Nazis into his government.
3. Schuschnigg decided to hold a referendum to see if the Austrian people wanted Anschluss with Germany.
4. Hitler forced Schuschnigg to resign and replaced him with an Austrian Nazi who invited German troops into Austria.
5. In March, German troops marched into Austria and the Anschluss was announced.
6. The Nazis organised a referendum; 99 per cent of the people voted in favour.

Britain and France protested, but did nothing – another example of appeasement. Some people argued that it was natural for Germany to be united.

Step 3

The crisis over the Sudetenland 1938

You will remember that Czechoslovakia had been created by the peace treaties at the end of the First World War. The part of Czechoslovakia on the border with Germany was called the Sudetenland. Most of the population were Germans.

Hitler financed and controlled the Sudeten-Germans who were led by Konrad Henlein. They began claiming that they were mistreated by the Czech Government and Hitler ordered the German army to be prepared to act.

It was at this stage that **Neville Chamberlain**, the British Prime Minister, decided to intervene. He persuaded the Czech President, **Benes**, to agree to self-government for the Sudeten-Germans. Hitler did not want the crisis settled this easily, however, and demanded that the Sudetenland become part of Germany. Benes refused.

The Munich Agreement

Chamberlain had three meetings with Hitler in all. The third one was in Munich in September 1938. Mussolini and Daladier, the French Prime Minister, were also present, but Russia was not invited – this made Stalin very bitter. The other country missing was Czechoslovakia. Benes was simply told what the other powers had decided to do with his country.

Hitler demanded the Sudetenland and Chamberlain, Mussolini and Daladier agreed. On the following day, Hitler promised Chamberlain that he did not want the rest of Czechoslovakia. Chamberlain returned to Britain waving the piece of paper on which Hitler had made this promise and claimed 'I believe it is peace for our time.'

Step 4

Germany takes the rest of Czechoslovakia

Czechoslovakia began to fall apart. She had no chance of defending herself. The Sudetenland had been her only defendable border. Poland and Hungary began to help themselves to parts of Czech territory and in March 1939 the German army marched in and took over the rest of Czechoslovakia.

Appeasement

Britain and France now changed their tactics and began to take a stronger line with Germany. Hitler now started to threaten Poland.

Britain and France began to speed up their rearmament programmes and promised to defend Poland if she was attacked.

Does this mean that appeasement had been a mistake? Historians have differed over this. See what you think.

Arguments in support of appeasement

- Britain had reduced her armed forces after the First World War and was too weak to fight Germany. It was best to appease Germany until Britain's armed forces had been built up again. Chamberlain was doing this. France was in the same position.
- Britain and France were afraid of communism spreading across Europe. They saw Hitler as a strong man who could stand up to the Soviet Union and communism.
- Most people could still remember the terrible things that happened in the First World War. Many people would try anything to avoid another war.
- Some people felt that Germany had been unfairly punished in the Treaty of Versailles. They thought that Germany should have some of her land back.

Arguments against appeasement

- Appeasement made Hitler feel he could get away with anything. Every time Britain and France failed to stand up to him he was encouraged to make more demands.
- When the Russians saw Britain and France appeasing Germany they were afraid that no one would come to their help if Germany invaded them. This encouraged them to reach an agreement with Germany – the Nazi–Soviet Pact of 1939. See below.
- Britain and France were fooled by Hitler. He didn't mean it when he promised that his latest conquest would be his last. By the time they realised this it was almost too late.

Step 5   The Nazi–Soviet Pact and the German invasion of Poland 1939

Fig. 5.3 A British cartoon about the Nazi–Soviet Pact of 1939. It shows Hitler and Stalin greeting each other over the body of Poland.

Hitler now hesitated before he made his next move. He was worried about having to fight a war on two fronts – Britain and France in the west, and Russia in the east. Britain and France started to talk with Russia about how they could work together against Germany but no one showed much urgency. (Stalin was still bitter about being left out of the Munich meeting.) Russia was also in talks with Germany and in August 1939 the Nazi–Soviet Pact was signed.

The Nazi–Soviet Pact

The public part of the pact was that:

- the two countries agreed not to attack each other

The secret part of the pact was that:

- Germany and Russia would share Poland between them

> **KEY POINT**
>
> The Nazi–Soviet Pact was the turning point. It made it possible for Hitler to carry out his plans. You could say it made it difficult for him not to continue with them. Was there no going back after this pact?

Some historians claim that Britain and France were to blame for Russia signing the Pact with Germany. They say that Britain and France had shown little interest in joining in an anti-German agreement with Russia, so Russia was forced to join with Germany.

The Nazi–Soviet Pact was crucial to Hitler's plans because it meant that he would not be faced with a war on two fronts. He did not even expect Britain and France to defend Poland. They had not stood up to him before, and what could they do about a country hundreds of miles away?

- On 1 September 1939 Germany invaded Poland.
- On 3 September Britain and France declared war on Germany.
- On 15 September Russia invaded Poland from the east.
- Poland was conquered within weeks and was divided up between Germany and Russia.

Reasons why war broke out in 1939

AQA B
OCR B
NICCEA

War did not break out for only one reason. It was the result of the combination of the following reasons.

- The peace settlements of 1919–1923 were flawed. They made Germany resentful. Sooner or later she would want revenge.
- The League of Nations was weak. By not standing up to Japan and Italy over Manchuria and Abyssinia it showed that countries could get away with aggression.
- The Depression led to extreme right-wing governments like Hitler's coming to power. It also led to some countries adopting aggressive foreign policies for economic reasons and to countries being more concerned about their own affairs than what was going on in the rest of Europe.
- Hitler must take a lot of the blame. He broke the Treaty of Versailles and used force to get want he wanted. The aggressiveness of Italy and Japan were also factors.
- Appeasement of Germany by Britain and France was also to blame. It led Hitler to believe he could get away with anything and encouraged him to be more aggressive.
- Britain, France and Russia failed to stand together against Germany. Britain and France were reluctant to ally with Russia because it was communist. This encouraged Russia to sign the Nazi–Soviet Pact with Germany, which made Hitler's invasion of Poland possible.

> **PROGRESS CHECK**
>
> Put these steps to war in the correct order and give each one a date.
>
> 1. The Nazi–Soviet Pact and the invasion of Poland
> 2. Germany sends troops into the Rhineland
> 3. Germany takes over Eastern Czechoslovakia
> 4. The Anschluss with Austria
>
> 1. Germany sends troops into the Rhineland 1936 2. The Anschluss with Austria 1938 3. German takes over the rest of Czechoslovakia 1939 4. The Nazi-Soviet Pact and the invasion of Poland 1939

Sample GCSE questions

1. Study the following sources

Source A: Hitler's aims in foreign policy

Like many Germans, Hitler wanted to abolish the Treaty of Versailles. Germany had stopped making reparations payments. Now Hitler wanted other parts of the Treaty changing as well. He wanted to expand German territory and unite all the Germans in Europe into one country. He wanted to expand German territory in Eastern Europe and Russia to create more Lebensraum (living space) for the German race.

From a textbook published in Britain in 2000.

Source B: The Hossbach Memorandum

Hitler stated that Lebensraum for Germans was to be found in Europe. The first aim must be to overrun Czechoslovakia and Austria and so secure Germany's eastern and southern borders.

From the minutes of a secret meeting between Hitler and his commanders held in November 1937.

(a) According to Source A, what were Hitler's aims in foreign policy? **[3]**

Hitler's aims were to abolish the Treaty of Versailles, and to make **Germany bigger. He also wanted living space for the expanding German** *population.*

> *There are only three marks for this question. This means the examiner simply wants three points. These must come from Source A. You will not get any marks for aims that are not in Source A. Do not spend a lot of time writing extra information on each aim – you will not get extra marks. The answer given scores three out of three.*

(b) How reliable is Source B to an historian writing about Hitler's aims in foreign policy? Use Source B and your own knowledge to answer the question. **[6]**

This source is quite reliable about Hitler's aims in foreign policy. He did want Lebensraum for the Germans but he was willing to look outside Europe as well as inside. He thought Lebensraum could also be found in Russia and this is why he later invaded Russia. The source is right about Austria and Czechoslovakia. He united Germany with Austria and then he invaded Czechoslovakia. The source is not entirely reliable about this because he gained part of Czechoslovakia by negotiation at Munich rather than by force.

The other thing that makes me think the source might be reliable is that this was a secret meeting with his commanders. Hitler had no reason to lie to them. In fact, he wants them to achieve his aims, so he would tell them the truth.

> *In the first part of the answer knowledge of Hitler's aims and what he did is being used to test what the source is saying. This knowledge is used to support some things in the source, and to question others.*

> *In the second paragraph the nature of the source is considered – the fact that it is a secret meeting. Does this make it more likely or less likely to be reliable?*

Sample GCSE questions

(c) Was Hitler's foreign policy the most important reason for the outbreak of the Second World War? Explain your answer. **[10]**

> *Make sure you write about a number of causes, not just Hitler's foreign policy, and not just the cause which you think is the most important.*

There were several reasons for the outbreak of the Second World War and Hitler's foreign policy was just one of them. It is difficult to say if one was more important than another because they were all linked together and all led to each other. They each happened because the other causes were there.

The first cause was the Treaty of Versailles. This punished Germany so harshly that it meant she wanted revenge at some time. Most Germans would support as leader someone who promised to get their lands back and who would make Germany great again. Most Germans thought all German speakers should be united in the same country. However, Versailles had gone against this by putting a lot of Germans in other countries, such as Czechoslovakia. Germany also resented having her armed forced reduced. All this meant that sooner or later Germany would be challenging the peace settlement.

The Great Depression played a part because this led to Hitler gaining power in Germany. Hitler's foreign policy was governed by the Treaty of Versailles. Most of it was about undoing the terms of the treaty: rearmament, winning back territory, creating a Greater Germany. However, the Second World War only broke out because Britain and France had appeased Germany. They let Hitler get away with re-occupying the Rhineland and then uniting with Austria. When they also gave in over the Sudetenland Hitler was given the impression that they would never stand up to him. He thought he could get away with anything. If they had stood up to him earlier the Second World War may have been avoided.

> *Try to explain how one cause leads to another – how they are all connected. This answer shows how the Treaty of Versailles, Hitler's foreign policy, appeasement and the Nazi–Soviet Pact were all connected. They all helped bring about the outbreak of the war and so it is difficult to say that one was more important than the others.*

The final cause of the war was the Nazi–Soviet Pact. This made Hitler feel safe to invade Poland because he knew Russia would not go to war with him. Without the pact he may not have invaded Poland. It was the invasion of Poland that sparked off the war.

So Hitler's foreign policy was partly to blame, but other countries who let him carry out this policy are also to blame. All these causes were important. One was not more important than the others.

AQA Specimen Paper 1

> *You do not have to conclude that one cause was more important than the others. You can argue that they were all important and it is impossible to say that one was the most important.*

The following topics are covered in this chapter:

- The early war years and war outside Europe
- The defeat of Japan and Germany
- The Home Front in Britain

6.1 The early war years and war outside Europe

LEARNING SUMMARY

After studying this section you should understand:

- the reasons for German successes early in the war
- how Britain was able to survive in the early part of the war
- how the war spread outside Europe
- why Japan and America entered the war

Early German successes

AQA B
EDEXCEL A
NICCEA

For the events leading up to the German invasion of Poland see pages 61–65.

For the Nazi–Soviet Pact see pages 64–65.

The success of Blitzkrieg depended on surprise and speed. The Luftwaffe destroyed the enemy airforce while it was still on the ground and bombed transport systems. Parachutists landed behind enemy lines to capture important targets and tanks and armoured cars smashed through enemy defences.

Poland defeated

On 1 September 1939 Germany invaded Poland from the west and on 15 September Russia invaded from the east. Poland was swiftly defeated by the German tactics of **Blitzkrieg** (lightning war). Britain and France could do little. On 3 October Poland surrendered.

This was followed by the '**Phoney War**' in the winter of 1939–1940, so called because each side waited for the other to make a move. As a result, nothing happened.

German successes in the west

In April 1940 Germany, using Blitzkreig tactics, invaded Denmark and Norway. This led to Winston Churchill replacing Neville Chamberlain as British Prime Minister in May 1940.

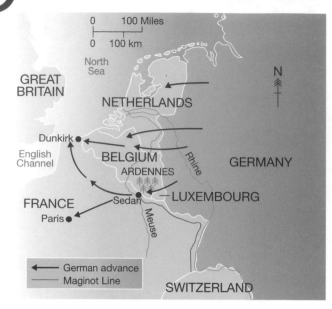

Fig. 6.1 German invasion of France.

On 10 May German troops attacked Holland, Belgium and France using Blitzkrieg tactics. A total of 340,000 British and French troops were forced to retreat to **Dunkirk** on the edge of the English Channel. They were at the mercy of the German army but for some reason Hitler did not attack them with his army and 300,000 troops were rescued by a fleet of all types of boats and ships from Britain. Although Dunkirk was a defeat for the Allies (Britain was now in no position to help defend France), Churchill used it for propaganda purposes to boost morale. The rescue of the troops by small boats led to the phrase 'Dunkirk spirit'.

The German invasion of France continued and in June 1940 France surrendered. Britain stood alone.

Hitler made a mistake in not using his armies to finish off the Allied troops at Dunkirk.

Examiner's tip: Dunkirk can be seen as both a defeat and a triumph for Britain. Be ready to argue both sides.

Reasons for German success

● Blitzkrieg tactics.
● Neither Britain nor France was ready to intervene with large numbers of troops to help Poland.
● Norwegian forces were not mobilised and Norwegian Nazis, led by Quisling, helped the invaders.
● By invading France through Belgium the German army by-passed the French defences of the Maginot Line which had been built along the French–German border.

The survival of Britain

AQA B
EDEXCEL A
NICCEA

The Battle of Britain July–September 1940

Hitler now planned to invade Britain (Operation Sealion). This would involve a fleet of barges carrying troops across the English Channel. First, however, Germany needed to win control of the air.

From July to September 1940 the two airforces fought for control of the skies in the Battle of Britain. The Luftwaffe tried different tactics: first bombing convoys in the Channel, then airfields and then factories. German losses were heavier than British, but by September Britain was short of planes and pilots, and six out of seven major airfields in the South-East of England were badly damaged. Not realising this, the Germans switched tactics to bombing London and other large cities. Hitler had given up his plans for an invasion. The Germans had lost 1,389 planes, the British 792.

Reasons for the victory of the RAF in the Battle of Britain

● The British Spitfires and Hurricanes were more manoeuvrable than the German Messerschmidts. The Messerschmidts only had enough fuel for 90 minutes flying.
● The Germans failed to bomb the British radar stations which told the RAF where and when German attacks were coming.

- The Germans did not realise how close to defeat the RAF was in September. They were worried about their own losses and made the mistake of calling off the attacks on airfields and factories, and turning to night bombing of cities instead.
- British factories produced new planes more quickly than German factories.
- The skill and bravery of the British pilots surpassed that of the Germans.

<aside>The Battle of Britain was an important turning point in the war. It meant that there would be no quick, total German victory in the west. If Hitler invaded Russia he would have to fight on two fronts.</aside>

The Battle of the Atlantic

Britain depended on food, oil and raw materials from the USA. Germany used U-boats, often hunting in 'wolfpacks', to sink convoys of merchant ships. They calculated that if they sank 150 merchant ships every month for a year, Britain would have to surrender. Churchill later wrote that 'The only thing that ever really frightened me during the war was the U-boat peril.'

In 1942 and early 1943 losses were heavy (in 1942 about 140 merchant ships were sunk each month). Later in 1943, however, the successes of the U-boats declined. They lost the Battle of the Atlantic.

Reasons for the British victory in the Battle of the Atlantic

- Merchant ships sailed in convoys which could be protected by warships.
- British warships and aircraft began to use radar to tell them where the submarines were. The British also broke German codes allowing them to follow the movement of the submarines. By the end of the war warships and planes had sunk over 750 German U-boats.
- The Allies were building merchant ships more quickly than the Germans could sink them.

The war spreads

AQA B
EDEXCEL A
NICCEA

Greece

In September 1940 Mussolini invaded Greece but the Italian forces were driven back. Both Hitler and the Allies sent troops. The Allies were overrun and retreated to the island of Crete which was captured by German parachutists in June 1940.

Africa

In September 1940 Mussolini also invaded Egypt in North Africa. British, Indian, Australian and New Zealand troops pushed the Italians out of Egypt and back into Libya. Hitler had to come to Italy's aid again. He sent **Rommel**, one of his best generals. In 1942 Rommel pushed the Allied armies deep into Egypt, threatening the Suez Canal and the Gulf oil fields.

The **Battle of El Alamein**, in October 1942, was the turning point in Africa. **General Montgomery's** Eighth Army defeated Rommel and pushed them out of Egypt and deep into Libya. Later in 1942 Allied troops landed in Algeria and soon the fighting in North Africa was over. In 1943 the Allies invaded Italy from North Africa.

<aside>The Battle of El Alamein was one of the turning points in the war.</aside>

Operation Barbarossa and the German invasion of Russia

For more information about Lebensraum see page 60.

Although Hitler had signed the Nazi–Soviet Pact with Stalin in 1939 he always planned to invade Russia. Hitler wanted:

- Lebensraum for the German people
- to destroy communism
- resources such as wheat in the Ukraine and oil in the Caucasus

Fig. 6.2 A British cartoon from July 1941, about the German invasion of Russia.

In June 1941 Hitler launched **Operation Barbarossa** and invaded Russia. Blitzkrieg tactics were used and by the winter of 1941–1942 the German armies had advanced deep into Russia. However, then the Russian winter struck and the advance slowed to a halt. Conditions were terrible with: sub-zero temperatures and snow. The German soldiers were not equipped for these conditions. They were held up by Russian resistance at Leningrad and Moscow.

In the spring of 1942 the Germans advanced again but were held up by stubborn Russian resistance at **Stalingrad**. Then they were again hit by the winter. In January 1943 the German army at Stalingrad (100,000 men) surrendered. The Russians began to push the Germans back and in June 1944 all German armies had been driven from Russia. A total of 20 million Russians (soldiers and civilians) died.

Reasons for the German defeat

Stalingrad was an important turning point in the war. Russian resistance was crucial to the outcome of the war. A total of 75 per cent of German forces were in Russia and this gave the Allies time to prepare for a major offensive in the west.

1. The Allied offensive in Greece held up the German invasion of Russia. This meant that when the Germans did attack (in June) the dreadful Russian winter was not far off.
2. The Germans found it difficult to keep their armies supplied over such vast distances. This was made harder by the 'scorched earth' policy of the Russians (destroying everything as they retreated).
3. The harsh winter of 1941 halted the German advance.
4. The Russian armies and the Russian people showed stubborn resistance.

The Russian armies then went on to drive Germany from Eastern Europe.

America and the war with Japan

AQA B
EDEXCEL A
NICCEA

Causes of the war with Japan

Japanese expansion

For the Japanese invasion of Manchuria see pages 54–55.

Japan had already conquered Manchuria and by 1941 had invaded deep into China. In 1941 Japan invaded Indo-China. Japan needed supplies of coal, oil, tin and other raw materials. America was very worried about Japanese advances in these areas.

Fig. 6.3 Map of Japanese expansion.

The Japanese army was virtually in control of Japan. Its leaders admired dictators like Hitler and in 1936 signed an agreement with him.

The reaction of America

The USA had important trading links with China and could not afford to let Japan dominate the area. In 1941 America demanded that Japan withdraw from China and Indo-China, and stopped trading with Japan. This was particularly serious for Japan because it depended on America for 80 per cent of its oil.

Pearl Harbor December 1941

However, Japan was not prepared to withdraw from China and Indo-China.

It decided to launch a surprise attack on the US naval base at **Pearl Harbor** in Hawaii. If the US navy in the Pacific could be destroyed, Japan could conquer the whole of the Pacific and South-East Asia.

In the attack most of the US fleet and 120 aircraft were destroyed, and 2,400 Americans were killed.

> Pearl Harbor was an important turning point in the war.

The results of Pearl Harbor

Pearl Harbor was important because:

● America declared war on Japan next day
● Germany and Italy declared war on America three days later

6.2 The defeat of Japan and Germany

> **LEARNING SUMMARY**

After studying this section you should understand:

● *why Japan lost the war*
● *why Germany lost the war*

The defeat of Japan

The Japanese quickly made advances in 1941. The Philippines, Malaya, Singapore, and parts of Burma all fell.

> The Battle of Midway Island was an important turning point in the war.

In 1942 the tide turned with **the Battle of Midway Island**: the US fleet sank four Japanese aircraft carriers. The Japanese position in the Pacific was seriously weakened.

Fig. 6.4 Hiroshima after the bomb.

In Hiroshima about 70,000 people died within minutes of the bomb being dropped.

- In 1943 the American army began to conquer one Pacific island after another ('island hopping'). American casualties were high but the Japanese were in retreat.
- In June 1944 British and Indian troops defeated Japan in Burma.
- In 1944–1945 America won the Philippines back. Only Japan was left.

Hiroshima and Nagasaki

Only Japan was left to conquer. The Americans were worried that a land invasion of Japan would result in very high casualties. Instead, **Harry Truman**, the American President, decided to use atomic bombs for the first time. In August one was dropped on the city of **Hiroshima**, and a few days later one on **Nagasaki**. On 14 August 1945 Japan surrendered.

The defeat of Germany

AQA B
EDEXCEL A
NICCEA

By June 1944 Britain and France were ready to launch their offensive in Europe. This was now possible because of the following factors.

- Germany had suffered massive losses in Russia and was being pushed back.
- In July 1943 British and American troops had landed in Italy. By April 1945 Italy had fallen.
- Over 3 million British, Canadian and American troops were in southern Britain ready to invade France. Five thousand ships were ready to transport them. Other preparations included 'mulberry' harbours which could be towed across the Channel, and a pipeline (Pluto) to be laid across the seabed of the Channel to supply fuel.

KEY POINT

Control of the skies and secrecy were vital elements of the successful D-Day landings. The Allies had control of the skies to protect the invasion fleet.

D-Day 6 June 1944

1. The landings were on five different beaches on a 60-mile stretch of the Normandy coast. German resistance was strong and casualties were high.
2. Within three weeks northern France had been liberated. On 25 August, Paris fell.
3. By September both France and Belgium had been freed from German control.
4. In December the Germans launched a counter-attack, 'The Battle of the Bulge'. The Allies were pushed back, but then recovered. Hitler had gambled everything on this attack: he lost 250,000 men and 600 tanks.
5. By April 1945 the Allies were entering Germany. However, the Russians, attacking from the east, reached Berlin first.
6. Hitler shot himself on 30 April and Germany surrendered on 7 May: VE Day.

Reasons for the defeat of Germany

1. Germany failed to defeat Britain in 1940 (the Battle of Britain).
2. Hitler attempted too much, particularly when he invaded Russia while he still had Britain to defeat.
3. Italy was a hindrance to Hitler. He kept having to use resources to support Mussolini's armies.
4. The longer the war went on the more Germany, Japan and Italy became short of essential supplies. The Allies, on the other hand, were being supplied by America.
5. The entry of America into the war was, at the end, decisive.

Crucial turning points

1940	The Battle of Britain prevented an invasion of Britain
1940–1943	The Battle of the Atlantic prevented Britain being starved of food and weapons
June 1941	Hitler's decision to invade Russia: a big mistake
December 1941	The Japanese bombing of Pearl Harbor: another mistake, bringing America into the war
1942	The Battle of Midway Island in the Pacific The Battle of El Alamein in North Africa The defeat of the German army at Stalingrad

6.3 The Home Front in Britain

LEARNING SUMMARY

After studying this section you should understand:

- *preparations by the British government*
- *evacuation and the Blitz*
- *new government powers*
- *rationing*

Early preparations by the government

AQA B
EDEXCEL A
WJEC A
NICCEA

Although the outbreak of war was not welcomed with enthusiasm as it had been in 1914, the government had already been making preparations.

- By 1939 1.5 million **Anderson shelters** had been distributed. These could be sunk into the ground in people's gardens.
- The Air Raid Precaution Act 1937. ARP teams were formed in towns. In 1938 (at the time of the Munich Crisis) the first air-raid shelters were built.
- In 1938 **gas masks** were issued to everyone.

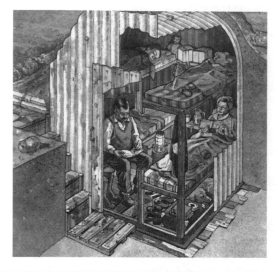

- **Conscription** – in April 1939 men aged 20–21 could be conscripted for the armed services. When war started in September conscription was extended to men aged 19–41. People working in essential jobs were not conscripted. In 1941 unmarried women had to join the armed or auxiliary services, or work in an essential industry.
- In July 1939 **'black-out'** instructions were issued telling people how to use blinds or blankets to hide the lights in their homes. The black-out was introduced two days before war was declared.

Fig. 6.5 An Anderson shelter.

Evacuation and the Blitz

AQA B
EDEXCEL A
WJEC A

German bombing of major towns and cities was expected, so during the first weekend in September 1939 a massive **evacuation** took place to reception areas (country areas where bombing was unlikely).

Fig. 6.6 Evacuees.

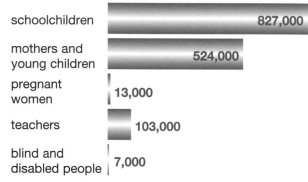

Fig. 6.7 Numbers of people evacuated.

schoolchildren	827,000
mothers and young children	524,000
pregnant women	13,000
teachers	103,000
blind and disabled people	7,000

The expected bombing did not come at first. Instead there was the 'Phoney War'. Then in September 1940 the **Blitz** began. During the night, wave after wave of bombs showered down on London, and then on other major cities like Liverpool, Glasgow, Coventry and Plymouth. Nearly half the evacuees had returned home by this time and had to be evacuated all over again.

As well as Anderson shelters, **Morrison shelters** were distributed. These were steel boxes, containing mattresses, which could be kept indoors. Many people sheltered in underground stations when there was an air raid.

By the time the Blitz ended in May 1941, 1.4 million people had been made homeless and 43,000 killed. The Germans had hoped to destroy British morale by the bombing. In fact, it had the opposite effect. People were determined not to be bombed into defeat. They volunteered as air-raid wardens, auxiliary fire-fighters, and for the Women's Voluntary Service, which looked after the injured.

The Local Defence Volunteers (later called the Home Guard or 'Dad's Army') was responsible for guarding the coast, protecting important buildings and fighting to defend the country if Germany invaded. 250,000 men volunteered. Their work was important because it meant the army could concentrate on fighting the war in other parts of the world.

The role of women

AQA B
EDEXCEL A
WJEC A
NICCEA

Percentage

Manufacture/repair of cars, aircraft

Local government fire service

Chemicals explosives

Farming

Banking insurance

National government service

1938
1944

Just as in the First World War women played a crucial part in the war effort. They worked in the auxiliary services, e.g. as nurses; the Women's Land Army was started again; and many women worked in industry. The figure shows how the role of women was changing.

Fig. 6.8 Women's part in the workforce 1938 and 1944.

New government powers

AQA B
EDEXCEL A
WJEC A
NICCEA

For the Defence of the Realm Act see page 23.

As in the First World War the government needed new powers to fight the war effectively.

- The Defence of the Realm Act from the First World War was renewed.
- The Emergency Powers Acts 1939 and 1940 gave the government powers to do almost anything.
  - German nationals and British Fascists were imprisoned without trial.
  - Newspapers were censored. The government wanted to make sure that people received its version of what was happening in the war. Posters, films and the radio were used.
- The government took control of industry, transport and the docks.

The leadership of Winston Churchill

AQA B
EDEXCEL A
WJEC A
NICCEA

Public morale in Britain was vital for the country to continue to resist Germany.

When Winston Churchill became Prime Minister in 1940, he formed a National Government and appointed people from all parties as ministers. A War Cabinet of five took the important decisions.

Churchill was a crucial factor in raising the morale of the British people. His brilliant speeches, heard over the radio, made it clear that defeat was not an option. He spoke to people in their own language and convinced them that they were going to win.

Rationing

AQA B
EDEXCEL A
WJEC A
NICCEA

Food rationing was introduced in 1940, clothes rationing in 1941. Both were in short supply because German U-boats were sinking many of the supply ships from America.

Most people felt that rationing was fair because it meant that everyone, rich and poor, were treated in the same way.

Fig. 6.9 Typical weekly food rations per person.

Bacon	6 oz
Cheese	4 oz
Butter	4 oz
Eggs	2
Milk	1 pint
Tea	3 oz
Sugar	12 oz
Sweets	3 oz
Dried milk	4 pints a week
Dried eggs	12 every eight weeks

Looking to the future

AQA B
EDEXCEL A
WJEC A
NICCEA

Winston Churchill lost the 1945 election. People wanted a fresh start after the war and were impressed by the Labour Party's promise to set up a Welfare State. Clement Atlee was the new Prime Minister.

During the war the government took on new responsibilities for people's welfare. Evacuation of inner-city children had made the middle-classes aware of the poverty that existed. As a result the government began to plan for a better Britain after the war. A Welfare State was planned.

● 1942 The **Beveridge Report**: five problems had to be overcome:
   WANT (poverty), IGNORANCE (lack of education), DISEASE (lack of proper health care), IDLENESS (unemployment), SQUALOR (poor housing)

The National Government, and later the Labour Government, which was elected in 1945, passed laws to tackle these problems and set up a Welfare State.

● 1944 The **Butler Education Act**: fees for secondary schools abolished; the school leaving age to be raised to 15 in 1947
● 1946 The **National Insurance Act**: improved benefits for the sick and unemployed; better old age pensions
● 1948 The **National Health Service** set up: free medical care for everyone

PROGRESS CHECK

1. When was the Phoney War?
2. Give three reasons why the RAF won the Battle of Britain.
3. What was the German plan to attack Russia called?
4. Name two ways in which Britain prepared for the war on the Home Front before war had begun.
5. What were the five problems identified by the Beveridge Report?

5. Want, ignorance, disease, idleness, squalor.
4. Gas masks issued, Anderson Shelters distributed.
3. Operation Barbarossa
attacks on airfields.
2. British fighters more manoeuvrable, Germans did not bomb radar stations, Germans called off
1. Winter 1939-40

Sample GCSE questions

Source A: A map showing the German invasion of the Soviet Union.

Source B: Text extract from a school textbook about the history of the Soviet Union in the twentieth century, published in Britain in 1991.

The Nazi–Soviet Pact was fragile and likely to break down when it suited either of the parties. There is no evidence that Stalin was preparing a war against Germany. It seems more likely that Hitler's long-term hatred of Bolshevism and wish to gain Lebensraum (living space) played the key role in his decision to attack the Soviet Union.

Source C: Text extract from a book about international relations published in Britain in 1997.

On 22 June 1941, Germany made a surprise attack on the Soviet Union. Operation Barbarossa was a three-pronged attack on the cities of Leningrad, Moscow and Stalingrad. The plan would lead to the destruction of the Soviet Union and would give Germany access to wheatfields of the Ukraine and the oilfields of the Caucasus. Germany would also gain living space.

Sample GCSE questions

Source D: Text extract from the diary of General Halder, August 1941. Halder was one of the German commanders leading the German invasion.

We have underestimated the Russian giant. At the start of the war, we reckoned that we would face about 200 enemy divisions. Now we have already counted 360. Time favours the Russians. They are near their own resources and we are moving farther away from ours. Our troops are spread out over an immense line and are subjected to the enemy's constant attacks.

Source E: A photograph showing Soviet troops in action against the Germans in 1941.

Source F: Extract from Stalin's radio broadcast to the Soviet people at the time of the German invasion in June 1941.

The enemy is cruel. They are out to seize our lands, our grain and oil. They are out to restore the role of landlords, to turn our people into slaves of Germany. If we are forced to retreat, the enemy must not be left a single engine, a single pound of grain or a gallon of fuel. All valuable property including grain and fuel that cannot be withdrawn must be destroyed without fail. In areas occupied by the enemy, guerrillas must be formed, sabotage groups must be organised to combat the enemy by blowing up bridges and roads.

Sample GCSE questions

These questions are about Operation Barbarossa, the German invasion of the Soviet Union in 1941. Look carefully at Sources A to F and then answer the questions.

(a)   Study Source A. What can you learn from this source about the aims of the German invasion of the Soviet Union?   **[4]**

From this source I can learn that the aims of the Germans were to capture wheatfields and oilfields to strengthen the German economy. The Germans also wanted to destroy the USSR because it was communist. This was why they aimed at the major cities of Leningrad, Moscow and Stalingrad.

> *This is only worth four marks so a short answer is all that is required. Make sure you give at least two aims. They must be ones you can support from the details of the map. Try and develop what you say about each aim by a little knowledge. This answer does all these things, but does not overdo them.*

(b)   Study Sources A, B and C. Does Source C support the evidence of Sources A and B? Explain your answer.   **[6]**

Source C does largely support the evidence of Sources A and B. Source C mentions a three-pronged attack on the main cities and the map in Source A shows exactly this. Source C says that the attack was a surprise attack and this supports Source B when it says that Stalin was not preparing for war on Germany - so the German attack would be a surprise for him. Source C also supports Source B about Hitler wanting living space. However, Source B says that the Nazi-Soviet Pact was fragile and likely to break down. This is not supported by Source C which says that the German attack was a surprise.

> *When you are comparing Source C with Sources A and B make sure you compare them point by point as this answer does. Do not write a summary of one source, and then a summary of another and claim that they are similar or different. Usually with this type of question there are both similarities and differences to be found. The similarities are easy to find, but the ways in which Source C disagrees with Sources A or B are harder to find. The answer does mention one.*

(c)   Study Sources D and E. How useful are these sources as evidence about the problems faced by the German armies in the Soviet Union?   **[8]**

Source D is very useful in telling us about the problems facing the German army. Halder is writing in his diary and is admitting that the Germans are having problems and have made mistakes so it is probably reliable. It tells us that there were more Russian divisions than they expected, and that the Germans are having problems keeping their long supply lines open. Halder, being an important general, would know this. Source E makes both sources useful in a way because it supports Source D in that it shows the Russians were well equipped and ready for action. They seem well prepared for the winter conditions. Of course, Source E could be a propaganda photograph to show people how strong the Russian army was. These two sources do not tell us everything about the problems, for example they do not mention the `scorched earth´ policy of the Russians.

> *This answer explains how the sources are useful. It explains what they tell us about the problems faced by the Germans. But it goes further than this: it also considers if the sources can be trusted. If they cannot, then they will not be very useful evidence about the German problems. The end of the answer is very good too, because it uses knowledge to explain how the sources do not tell us about all the problems the Germans faced, so their usefulness is limited.*

Sample GCSE questions

(d) Study all the sources. 'Operation Barbarossa failed because it was badly planned.' Use the sources and your own knowledge to explain whether you agree with this view.

Operation Barbarossa failed partly because it was badly planned. For example, the German soldiers were not properly equipped for the conditions they would meet in the Russian winter. They had expected to make faster progress and did not expect to be still fighting in the middle of the dreadful Russian winter. Source D admits that they had got their plans wrong when it says that they had underestimated Russia. Also the deeper the Germans went into Russia the more difficult they found it to supply their armies. They had hoped to have a 'Blitzkieg' war which would be over in a few months at the most.

However, it was not all due to bad planning. The Germans had planned to attack Russia earlier but had been held up by the fighting in Greece and Crete. The German plan had been to invade earlier and have the invasion finished before the winter started. Also, the Germans could not have known that the Russian armies would put up such stubborn resistance and that the people in the cities would hold out even after months of siege. They also did not know about the Russian 'scorched earth' policy described in Source F, which meant that when the Russians retreated they left nothing behind for the Germans to use.

This answer is a good one because it (i) uses information from the sources and knowledge that is not in the sources, and (ii) provides a balanced argument: reasons are given as to why it was badly planned, but other reasons outside the control of the Germans are also explained.

Edexcel Specimen Paper 2

7 The causes of the Cold War 1945–1949

The following topics are covered in this chapter:

- ● *The Yalta and Potsdam Conferences*
- ● *Rivalry in Europe 1945-1949*

7.1 The Yalta and Potsdam Conferences

LEARNING SUMMARY

After studying this section you will know:

- ● *the problems facing the victorious countries at the end of the war*
- ● *what was agreed, and not agreed, at Yalta and Potsdam*
- ● *the policies of the USSR in Europe 1945–49*

The problems

AQA B
EDEXCEL A
OCR B
NICCEA

Russia wanted to keep Germany weak and Britain and America did not want to make the same mistake as was made in the Treaty of Versailles

For the Treaty of Versailles see page 42.

Even before the war had ended America, Britain and Russia were meeting to decide the future of Europe.

They had to try and solve the following problems.

1. What to do about Germany.

2. What to do about the countries in Eastern Europe that had been occupied. Stalin wanted a barrier between him and Germany to ensure that Russia was never invaded again. He wanted land from Poland and control over Eastern Europe. Britain and the USA were not keen on Eastern Europe falling under communist control.

3. How to make sure that peace would last.

Yalta February 1945

AQA B
EDEXCEL A
OCR B
NICCEA

Fig. 7.1 Churchill, Roosevelt, Stalin at Yalta.

Yalta was the last time the 'Big Three' (Churchill, Roosevelt and Stalin) would meet. Roosevelt died later in the year.

What was agreed

- Germany would be demilitarised and war criminals would be punished.
- Germany would be divided into four zones. These would be under the control of Britain, France, Russia and the USA. Berlin (which was in the Russian zone) would also be divided into four.
- Russia would join the war against Japan.
- Countries in Eastern Europe would hold free elections for new governments.
- A new organisation called the **United Nations** would replace the League of Nations.

What was not agreed

They did not agree over Stalin's demand for Polish land, but they did agree on the general point that Eastern Europe would be 'a Soviet sphere of influence'.

> They managed to agree because they left so much vague, e.g. what did 'a Soviet sphere of influence' mean? What was meant by 'free elections'? This vagueness would lead to disagreements later.

Potsdam July–August 1945

AQA B
EDEXCEL A
OCR B
NICCEA

> At Yalta Churchill had often mediated between Stalin and Roosevelt. Now there was nobody able to do this.

The situation had now changed.

- Truman had become US President (he was more anti-communist than Roosevelt). Stalin and Truman were very suspicious of each other.
- During the conference, Churchill lost the general election in Britain and was replaced as Prime Minister by Clement Attlee.
- Russian armies occupied all the Eastern European countries and Stalin had already set up a communist government in Poland.
- Truman told Stalin about the American atom bomb. This made Stalin even more suspicious.

Disagreements at Potsdam

There was more disagreement than agreement at Potsdam.

- Because of the huge damage suffered by Russia in the war Stalin wanted to punish and weaken Germany so it could never threaten war again. He also wanted large reparations from Germany. Truman thought it would be a mistake to punish Germany too harshly: it would be repeating the mistakes made in 1919 in the Treaty of Versailles.
- Stalin wanted Eastern Europe to be communist and under his influence. Truman was very unhappy about this.

Agreements at Potsdam

The agreements were vague:

- the 6 million Germans in Eastern Europe should be resettled in Germany
- for reparations, each of the Allies could take what they wanted from their zone of Germany

Fig. 7.2 The Iron Curtain by 1950.

Examiner's tip: Make sure you can explain why less progress was made at Potsdam than at Yalta.

There was no final agreement over Eastern Europe. In fact, there was little to discuss. Russian troops controlled these countries and there was little Britain and America could do about this. The final division of Europe between east and west, between communist and non-communist, was largely decided by where the Russian and the American/British armies met at the end of the war.

This was the last meeting of the wartime allies. The USA and the USSR now viewed each other with total suspicion. Each feared the other. Britain and France were badly weakened by the war and it was clear that the USA and USSR would dominate world affairs in the near future.

Winston Churchill summed up the situation in a speech in 1946, 'From Stettin in the Baltic to Trieste in the Adriatic, an iron curtain has descended across the continent.'

PROGRESS CHECK

1. Name three problems that faced the victorious countries at the end of the war.
2. Name three things that were agreed at Yalta.
3. Briefly describe two ways in which the situation had changed at the time of the Potsdam meeting.
4. Who coined the term 'the Iron Curtain'?

1. What to do about Germany. Who was going to control the occupied countries of Eastern Europe. How to make sure that peace would last. 2. Choose from: Germany to be demilitarised, war criminals to be punished; Germany to be divided into four zones, as Berlin was; Russia to join the war against Japan; free elections in Eastern Europe; United Nations to replace the League of Nations. 3. Choose from: Truman replaced Roosevelt; Attlee replaced Churchill; Russian armies occupied Eastern Europe; Russians aware of the American atom bomb. 4. Winston Churchill.

7.2 *Rivalry in Europe 1945-1949*

LEARNING SUMMARY

After studying this section you will know:

● *what is meant by the term 'Cold War'*
● *the policies of the USA and the USSR 1945–1949*
● *what happened in the Berlin blockade and airlift*
● *the different views about who was responsible for the Cold War*

The Cold War

AQA B
EDEXCEL A
OCR B
NICCEA

The Cold War had begun. The USA and the USSR would:

● make threats to each other
● build up their armaments
● form alliances against each other

- try and win influence with other countries
- spread propaganda against each other

However, they would never actually go to war with each other.

The Cold War was really caused by the fear and mistrust between the two countries. The USA feared that Russia wanted to spread communism across Europe, and then the world. Russia feared another invasion from the west and thought America wanted to dominate Europe and the world. In 1945 Russia was much weaker than the USA.

The policies of the USSR and the USA 1945–1949

AQA B
EDEXCEL A
OCR B
NICCEA This section looks at the actions of Russia and America. It is difficult to decide who was causing the increased tension between them, and who was reacting to what the other was doing. The truth is that both countries were probably doing a bit of both.

Yugoslavia was unique: a communist country not under the control of the USSR. In 1948 Stalin expelled Yugoslavia from Cominform because Tito was too independent.

For the Marshall Plan see page 86.

Russia in Eastern Europe

Elections were held in the Eastern European countries but they were rigged to ensure communist victories. By 1948 most Eastern European countries had communist governments that were really controlled from Russia.
There were, however, some exceptions which are discussed below.

Yugoslavia

Marshal Tito had led the communist resistance to German occupation of Yugoslavia. He was popular and powerful, and established Yugoslavia as an independent communist state outside the control of Russia. In 1948 relations with Stalin finally broke down. Russia even moved troops to Yugoslavia's borders and cut off trade. Tito survived with the help of American economic aid.

Greece

In 1944 Greece set up a pro-Western government. This was opposed by Greek communists. Civil war broke out in 1944 and in 1946. America stepped in and the communists were defeated in 1949.

Cominform

In 1947 Stalin set up **Cominform**. This was in response to the **Marshall Plan**. It included communist parties all over Europe and was designed to make sure they all followed the same ideological line as Stalin.

America in Europe

As far as the Americans were concerned, Stalin was planning to take over Europe. This was probably not true. Stalin was determined to hold on to Eastern Europe but he had no plans for the rest of Europe.

> **KEY POINT** Remember, what America and Russia *feared* the other was planning was just as important as what they were *actually* planning.

The Truman Doctrine *1947*

Truman decided that American influence in Europe had to be strengthened. In 1947 he gave a speech in which he announced what became known as the Truman Doctrine:

'The United States would support (by economic or military aid) free peoples (meaning anti-communists) who were resisting armed minorities or outside pressures (meaning the USSR).'

Marshall Aid

The Truman Doctrine led to the Marshall Plan. General **George Marshall**, a member of the American Government, believed countries in Western Europe were close to economic collapse. Truman feared that people living in these conditions might turn to communism. He was also worried that a weak Western Europe would not be able to stand up to Russia.

In June 1947 Marshall announced the plan that was named after him.

Fig. 7.3 Churchill's Iron Curtain.

> **The American Congress thought that Truman was getting too involved in European affairs and, at first, opposed the Marshall Plan.**

> **Russia thought the Marshall Plan was an attempt by America to gain economic control of Europe.**

> **The first example of the Truman Doctrine in practice was American aid for the non-communist government in Greece.**

- Billions of dollars would be given to European countries to help them recover.
- They would have to agree to buy American goods and to allow American investment.
- Marshall asked the governments of Europe to get together to decide how much they wanted. Even Russia enquired but was not happy with the terms of membership. Stalin then banned all Eastern European countries from applying.
- When Truman asked the American Congress for the $17 billion required, it refused.
- However, the plan was saved in February 1948 when communists took over control in Czechoslovakia.
- This persuaded Congress of the threat from communism and they voted to give money for the plan.
- Marshall Aid did help European economies to recover. When the plan ended in 1952 industrial output was 35 per cent higher than it had been before the war.
- American industry also benefited from the Marshall Plan. Much of the money was spent buying materials and goods from America and this helped fuel the post-war boom in the US.

The Berlin blockade and airlift 1948–1949

> AQA B
> EDEXCEL A
> OCR B
> NICCEA

Causes of the blockade

America, Britain and France wanted their zones in Germany to recover economically and eventually to be unified into a new West Germany. They had included their zones in the Marshall Plan and economic recovery was under way. Stalin wanted Germany to remain weak. He did not want a strong West Germany emerging that could be a threat to Russia and the communist bloc.

In June 1948 a new currency, the Deutschmark, was introduced into the western zones to help economic recovery. It was then introduced into the western sectors of Berlin. This really annoyed Stalin who accused the West of interfering in East Germany (remember Berlin was in East Germany). The following events then took place.

Fig. 7.4 A divided Germany.

Blockade and airlift

- June 1948 Russia closed the roads, railways and waterways that linked the western sectors of Berlin with West Germany. The blockade of Berlin had started. If supplies could not be got to the people in Berlin, America, Britain and France would have to withdraw.
- Attempts to break the blockade could end in war – and the Russians had far more troops on the ground.
- The solution was to airlift supplies to Berlin. Airlifts started in June 1948 and put the ball back into Russia's court: she would have to fire the first shot.
- The airlift supplied Berlin with 1.5 million tonnes of supplies over 318 days.

- In July 1948 American B29 bombers were sent to bases in Britain. The Russians were not sure if they were carrying nuclear weapons.
- On 12 May 1949 the Russians lifted the blockade.

The consequences of the Berlin Crisis

- Relations between America and Russia were worse than ever.
- Germany was divided into the Federal Republic of Germany (West Germany) and the German Democratic Republic (East Germany).
- During the crisis Western countries, including America, formed the **North Atlantic Treaty Organisation (NATO).** This was a military alliance. If a member of the alliance was attacked the others would help them.
- In 1955 the USSR responded with its own alliance. With the communist countries of Eastern Europe (not Yugoslavia) it formed the **Warsaw Pact**. Europe was now divided into two armed camps.

Who was to blame for the Cold War?

Examiner's tip: This is a difficult question to answer – and there is no 'right' answer. The examiners will be looking for how well you support your arguments. Even if you have made up your mind who was largely to blame, you should explain how the other side also contributed to the tension.

- At Yalta Britain and America did agree that Eastern Europe should be a Soviet 'sphere of influence'. However, what this meant was left vague.
- At Yalta it was agreed that 'free' elections should be held in Eastern Europe. Russia made sure these were rigged in favour of communists.
- There is no evidence that Stalin wanted control beyond Eastern Europe. Some historians believe he just wanted a 'safety barrier' between Russia and Western Europe. Russia had been invaded twice in the last 30 years.
- The Marshall Plan was seen by Russia as an American attempt to control Europe.
- Russia was worried by the American atom bomb.
- America was genuinely worried that Russia wanted to spread communism across Europe.
- America was worried by the large number of troops the Russians had in Eastern Europe.
- The most important point is that each side mistrusted the other. They suspected each other of ambitions of world control that neither had.

Exam practice questions

1.

(a) What was agreed at the Potsdam Conference 1945? **(4)**

....

....

....

....

....

....

....

(b) Explain why the USA introduced the Marshall Plan. **(6)**

....

....

....

....

....

....

....

....

(c) 'The most important cause of the Cold War was the suspicion and rivalry
between Truman and Stalin.' Do you agree with this statement? **(10)**

....

....

....

....

....

....

....

....

....

OCR Specimen Paper 1

Tension and détente 1950–1981

The following topics are covered in this chapter:

- **The Korean War 1950–1953**
- **The Berlin Wall 1961**
- **The Cuban Missile Crisis 1962**
- **The Vietnam War**
- **Attempts at détente 1953–81**

8.1 The Korean War 1950–1953

LEARNING SUMMARY

After studying this section you will know:

- **the causes of the Korean War**
- **the main events of the war**
- **the results of the war**

The causes of the Korean War

AQA B
NICCEA

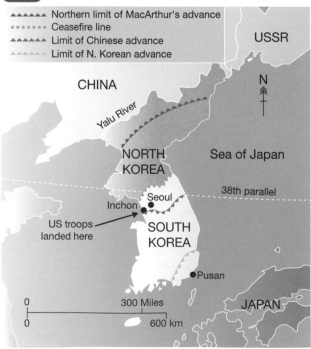

▲▲▲▲▲▲ Northern limit of MacArthur's advance
∙∙∙∙∙∙∙ Ceasefire line
▲▲▲▲▲ Limit of Chinese advance
▲▲▲▲▲ Limit of N. Korean advance

USSR

CHINA

N

Yalu River

NORTH KOREA

Sea of Japan

Seoul · 38th parallel
Inchon ·
US troops landed here

SOUTH KOREA

· Pusan

0 ____ 300 Miles
0 ____ 600 km

JAPAN

Fig. 8.1 North and South Korea.

Intervention in Korea was carried out with UN support, but it was really an American attempt at stopping communism from spreading.

The tension between communist and non-communist states was not limited to Europe and in 1950 it led to war in Korea.

Korea was divided into two states: North Korea was communist and supported by Russia; South Korea had an anti-communist dictatorship and was supported by America. The two Koreas were divided by the 38th parallel. Both Korean Presidents claimed to be ruler of the whole of Korea.

In 1950 North Korea invaded South Korea. The United Nations asked its members to help stop the war. The USA immediately sent troops. They were followed by troops from 16 other countries. However, the American army, led by **General MacArthur**, played the most important role and made the decisions. A total of 50 per cent of the army and 86 per cent of the navy was provided by America. MacArthur took orders from Truman, not from the UN.

Make sure you can explain the 'Domino Theory'. You will come across it again in this chapter.

America saw the invasion by North Korea as another example of the spread of communism which had to be stopped. America was worried about the **'domino effect'**: if one country fell to communism, this would trigger other countries to fall. Another reason for America's concern was that in 1949 China (just north of Korea) had become communist.

Fig. 8.2

The main events of the war

AQA B
NICCEA

1. The North Koreans made advances in South Korea.
2. September 1950: MacArthur landed at Inchon.
3. October 1950: the UN approved an American invasion of North Korea and the unification of Korea. Americans troops invaded North Korea the same day.
4. MacArthur's forces advanced through North Korea towards the Korea-China border.
5. November 1950: Chinese troops poured into North Korea and drove MacArthur back.
6. MacArthur asked Truman to use the atomic bomb and wanted to invade China. In April 1951 MacArthur was sacked by Truman.
7. June 1951: a stalemate had developed around the 38th parallel.
8. 1953: an armistice was signed and Korea remained divided along the 38th parallel.

Results of the Korean War

AQA B
NICCEA

- America realised that it could not take on China with its massive population. From now on American policy was to **contain** the spread of communism rather than to try and defeat it.

> **KEY POINT**
> American policy now changes to one of *containing* communism.

- The Korean War showed how easy it was for a regional conflict to suddenly escalate and nearly cause a world war.

- Russia accused the USA of using the UN for its own purposes.

PROGRESS CHECK

1. Name two ways in which South and North Korea differed.
2. How did China play an important part in the war?
3. Give three results of the war.

1. North Korea was communist and supported by Russia. South Korea was anti-communist and supported by America. 2. It prevented America from conquering North Korea. It led to a stalemate on the original border between North and South Korea. 3. America decided to contain communism rather then try and defeat it. The war showed how easily a regional conflict could escalate. America was accused of exploiting the UN.

8.2 The Berlin Wall 1961

LEARNING SUMMARY

After studying this section you will know:

- *why Berlin was a cause of tension between East and West*
- *why the Russians built the Berlin Wall*

Berlin: a cause of tension

AQA B
EDEXCEL A
OCR B
NICCEA

For the earlier crisis over Berlin and the Berlin Blockade, see pages 86–87.

The city of Berlin continued to cause tensions between Russia and America. You will remember that capitalist West Berlin was in the middle of communist East Germany. There had already been one crisis over Berlin (the Berlin Blockade in 1948–1949). The Russians found it difficult to accept this outpost of capitalism in communist territory. During 1959–1961 Khrushchev made several demands that the Western powers leave Berlin. They refused. In August 1961, East German soldiers put up a barbed-wire barrier dividing East and West Berlin. This was soon replaced by a wall – the Berlin Wall. Nobody was allowed to move between East and West Berlin. This meant that families were suddenly divided. It even stopped some people going to their place of work. East German soldiers guarded the wall and shot anyone who tried to cross to West Berlin.

Reasons why the Russians built the Berlin Wall

AQA B
EDEXCEL A
OCR B
NICCEA

- They regarded West Berlin as a '**listening post**' for America right in the middle of communist territory.
- Living standards in West Berlin were much higher than in East Berlin. While East Berliners could travel to West Berlin they could see how people were better off under capitalism.
- Many of the most educated and highly skilled people in East Berlin were defecting to West Berlin. The East could not afford to lose these people, e.g. scientists, teachers and engineers.

Berlin remained a source of tension between East and West. In 1963 Kennedy showed his support for the people of West Berlin by visiting the city and making his famous '**Ich bin ein Berliner**' speech.

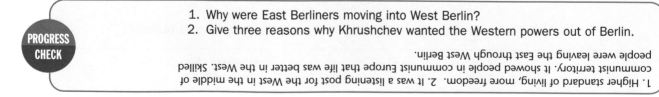

PROGRESS CHECK

1. Why were East Berliners moving into West Berlin?
2. Give three reasons why Khrushchev wanted the Western powers out of Berlin.

1. Higher standard of living, more freedom. 2. It was a listening post for the West in the middle of communist territory. It showed people in communist Europe that life was better in the West. Skilled people were leaving the East through West Berlin.

8.3 The Cuban Missile Crisis 1962

LEARNING SUMMARY

After studying this section you will know:

- *the long- and short-term causes of the crisis*
- *the main events of the crisis*
- *the results of the crisis*

To understand the Cuban Missile Crisis it is necessary to consider both the long- and short-term causes.

Long-term causes

AQA B
EDEXCEL A
OCR B
NICCEA

The Cuban Revolution and her worsening relations with America were the long-term causes of the crisis.

America had become heavily involved in the island of Cuba. It supported the dictator **Batista** and had a naval base there. American businessmen owned much of the industry in Cuba and made huge profits.

However, most Cubans lived in poverty. Batista's rule had degenerated into repression and gangsterism. In 1959 **Fidel Castro** overthrew Batista and set up what looked to the Americans like a communist regime. Relations between Cuba and America grew gradually worse.

Cuban exiles fled to Miami where they plotted the downfall of Castro.

↓

Castro nationalised a lot of the land in Cuba.

↓

America refused to sell arms to Cuba.

↓

In 1960 Russia began buying Cuban sugar. This had previously been bought by the USA.

↓

Eisenhower ordered the CIA to start training the Cuban exiles for a future invasion of Cuba.

↓

Cuba started to buy arms from Russia.

↓

America tried to stop Western countries selling oil to Cuba.

↓

August 1960: Castro nationalised hundreds of US companies.

↓

October 1960: the USA stopped trading with Cuba.

↓

January 1961: the USA broke off diplomatic relations with Cuba.

> Some historians think that the hostile actions of America simply pushed Cuba into the arms of Russia. They claim Castro had no choice.

The Bay of Pigs

AQA B
EDEXCEL A
OCR B
NICCEA

When Kennedy became President in 1961 there were already plans for Cuban exiles to invade Cuba. The invasion took place in April 1961. A total of 1,400 men landed at the Bay of Pigs.

The whole affair was a disaster. The Cuban people did not support them and they were easily defeated. Everyone knew America was behind the invasion and it pushed Castro even more into the arms of Russia.

These events show how relations between Cuba and America had deteriorated since Castro had come to power.

Short-term causes

AQA B
EDEXCEL A
OCR B
NICCEA

Short-term causes sparked off the crisis. Feeling more threatened than ever by America, Castro turned to Russia for support. Russia, meanwhile, was feeling threatened by US nuclear missiles in Europe and Turkey.

Fig. 8.3 The missile threat from Cuba.

Examiner's tip:
Be ready to argue why you think Khrushchev put missiles on Cuba. Was he justified?

Russia started to install nuclear missiles in Cuba – just 100 miles away from the US coast. The missiles were medium-range – able to reach most of the major cities in the USA. On 16 October 1962 two U-2 spy planes brought back photographs of the missile bases in Cuba.

Why did Russia put missiles on Cuba?

1. As something to bargain with. Russia could demand that America withdraw her missiles from Turkey, or demand that the Western powers withdraw from Berlin.
2. Khrushchev knew Russia was weaker than America and thought missiles on Cuba would even things up.
3. To defend Cuba against America.
4. To test the new President, Kennedy.

Main events of the crisis

AQA B
EDEXCEL A
OCR B
NICCEA

Kennedy had several options. What he decided was crucial because the world was close to nuclear war.

Examiner's tip:
Make sure you are able to explain the advantages and disadvantages of each of the options.

Do nothing	This would make America look weak and the missiles could be used at any time by Russia.
Use an air attack to destroy the bases	Russia might retaliate, and there was no guarantee all the bases would be destroyed.
Invade Cuba	This would get rid of Castro and the missiles, but might lead to all-out war.
Blockade Cuba, stopping more missiles arriving	Without using force, this would show that the USA would not tolerate the missiles, and would give Russia a way out of the crisis.

Kennedy decided on option 4. On 22 October 1962 he announced:

● a naval blockade of Cuba – Soviet ships would be stopped and searched to prevent any more missiles reaching Cuba

● all missiles in Cuba should be removed

Khrushchev now had to decide what to do.

24 October	Russian ships approaching Cuba turned round, but work on the missile bases continued.
26 October	Khrushchev offered to destroy the bases if America promised it would not attack Cuba, and if the blockade was lifted.
27 October	Khrushchev demanded that American missiles in Turkey be removed.
27 October	Kennedy decided to accept Khrushchev's first offer.
28 October	Khrushchev agreed. Kennedy also secretly agreed to take American missiles out of Turkey some time in the future.

Results of the crisis

AQA B
EDEXCEL A
OCR B
NICCEA

The crisis brought the world close to nuclear war. This had positive consequences because it made Russia and America realise how easily such a war could begin. This led to the following measures.

1. Both sides were now more ready to settle their differences by talking. The first evidence of this was when they set up a **telephone hotline** between them to make it easy for the two leaders to contact each other.

2. In 1963 they signed a **Nuclear Test Ban Treaty** which limited tests of nuclear weapons.

3. Cuba remained a communist country on America's doorstep. However, the nuclear missiles had gone and Cuba was no longer a threat to the USA.

4. President Kennedy's reputation was strengthened. He had shown he could stand up to the Russians.

Examiner's tip:
You need to be able to discuss who won and who lost in the Cuban Missile Crisis. You must have reasons to support your views.

5. The results for Khrushchev were mixed. He could claim that he had helped maintain peace, and that American missiles in Turkey would be removed. However, some people in Russia did not like the fact that he had caused the crisis and had then backed down. In 1964 he was sacked.

The Cuban Missile Crisis actually led to improved relations between Russia and America.

PROGRESS CHECK

1. Give two reasons why Soviet missiles were a threat to America.
2. List the options Kennedy had in reacting to the discovery of the missiles.
3. Give two results of the Cuban Missile Crisis.

1. Choose from: Cuba close to America; Cuba communist; the missiles could reach all major American cities. 2. To do nothing; to launch an air attack on the bases; to invade Cuba; to set up a blockade around Cuba. 3. Choose from: the telephone hotline; both sides realised how easily a nuclear war could start; improved relations between East and West.

8.4 The Vietnam War

LEARNING SUMMARY

After studying this section you will know:

● why America got involved in Vietnam
● why America lost the war

Reasons why America got involved in Vietnam

AQA B
EDEXCEL A
OCR B
NICCEA

Fig. 8.4 Vietcong strategic advantages.

1. In 1954 the French gave up trying to hold on to their empire in Indo-China. Vietnam had been part of this empire. It was divided into two. North Vietnam was under the communist government of **Ho Chi-Minh**. South Vietnam had a government that was friendly to the West. There was supposed to be an election in 1956 to choose a government for the whole of Vietnam. However, the Americans were against the election taking place because they thought the communists would win. They were afraid that if Vietnam became communist, other states would follow (the domino effect, see page 90).

2. The **Vietcong** (communist guerrillas) fought to overthrow the government of South Vietnam. They were helped by North Vietnam, which sent supplies down the Ho Chi Minh Trail. In 1955 the Americans started to support the government of the South.
In 1961 Kennedy increased this support by sending military advisers. **Johnson** had to fight an election in 1964 to remain President and thought a tough policy towards the communists in Vietnam would go down well with the electors.

3. In 1964 an American destroyer was attacked by North Vietnamese patrol boats. This persuaded Congress to support the sending of more troops to Vietnam. In 1964 President Johnson sent 23,000. By 1967 there were 500,000 American troops in Vietnam.

Why America lost the war

AQA B
EDEXCEL A
OCR B
NICCEA

The tactics used by the Vietcong

The Vietcong used **guerrilla** tactics. They rarely fought large battles. They lived off the land and disappeared among the ordinary people, waiting to strike when the time was right. They used booby traps and ambushes. They knew the countryside and could melt away into it.

The Americans could not tell who were innocent villagers and who were Vietcong. Many of the villagers supported and hid the guerrillas.

In January 1968 the communists launched the **Tet Offensive**: they attacked Saigon and hundreds of other towns in South Vietnam. They were eventually driven back, and in one sense the offensive was a defeat, but it sent a major shock through the American government. The generals requested more troops. When the news filtered out in America there was a public outcry. Johnson announced he would not run for the presidency again and in May 1968 peace talks began in Paris.

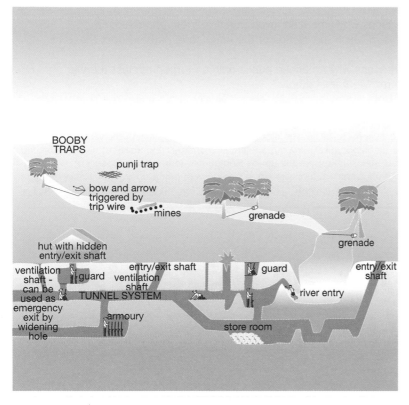

Fig. 8.5 Vietcong tunnel system.

The tactics used by the Americans

The Americans were fighting in a foreign country they did not know or understand. They were easy targets. They fought a different kind of war to the Vietcong. They depended on technology: bombers, gunships, heavily armoured troops. The methods used by the Americans – bombing villages, search-and-destroy missions, chemicals like napalm – lost them the support of the Vietnamese villagers. It gradually became clear that America would not win a military victory.

> The Americans did not adapt their tactics to the conditions in South Vietnam.

Opposition to the war in America

As the war dragged on and the number of American casualties grew, so did opposition to the war. At first this was limited to students who had been drafted into the army. However, as more and more parents received the news that their sons were dead (by 1968 over 36,000 Americans had been killed), opposition spread. Americans could see on their TV screens what was happening.

Nixon, the new President, had promised to reduce the number of Americans fighting in Vietnam. In 1969, however, he ordered the bombing of Cambodia, where the Vietcong had established some of their bases. The anti-war protests in America grew. Events like the shooting of four demonstrators at Kent State University and the massacre of Vietnamese civilians at **My Lai** made matters worse. The scale of the opposition to the war made it impossible for Nixon to continue American involvement.

> This was another example of the Domino Theory. Remember, this had influenced American thinking over Korea.

Nixon began to pull troops out and started a policy of **Vietnamisation** (the South Vietnam army fighting the Vietcong by itself). In 1973 a ceasefire was agreed, but the fighting continued. In 1975 North Vietnam and the Vietcong had conquered South Vietnam and united the country under communism.

1. Give three reasons why American involvement in Vietnam increased.
2. State two ways in which the tactics of the Americans differed from those of the Vietcong.
3. Name three reasons why American public opinion turned against the war.
4. Explain the term 'Vietnamisation'.

1. Choose from: the domino theory; fear of communism spreading; the threat to the government of South Vietnam; Johnson trying to win votes in the election; the attack on the American destroyer. 2. Choose from: use of technology; search-and-destroy missions; heavy bombing; use of napalm. 3. Choose from: high American casualties; the war was dragging on and going badly; the terrible scenes seen on television; the My Lai massacre; the killing of students at Kent State University. 4. To hand over the military effort to the South Vietnamese and help them to defend themselves. Withdrawal of most American troops

8.5 Attempts at détente 1953–1981

After studying this section you will know:

● *why both sides wanted détente*
● *details of the arms race*
● *how détente continued in the 1970s and 1980s*
● *the reasons détente came to end in the 1980s*

Reasons for détente

AQA B
EDEXCEL A
NICCEA

As you go through this section be careful to list examples of relations between Russia and America improving, and examples of them getting worse.

We have seen that the Cuban Missile Crisis helped to bring the two superpowers closer together. However, this process had begun before the crisis.

1953	Stalin died and was replaced by Khrushchev.
1953	Eisenhower replaced Truman as American President.
1955	Eisenhower and Khrushchev met at the Geneva Conference. They agreed to reduce Cold War tensions.
1956	Khrushchev rejected the polices of Stalin and called for '**peaceful co-existence**' between East and West.

The arms race

AQA B
EDEXCEL A
NICCEA

Despite both sides having enough nuclear arms to destroy the world several times, both continued to make more and better weapons. Each side tried to outdo the other. For most of the period after the Second World War America had the advantage.

● America developed the atom bomb first (during the Second World War). This gave it a start in the race, and it kept ahead for a long time.

- America had European bases from which its bombers could threaten the East with nuclear weapons. Although Russia was stronger in terms of land forces, its bombers could not reach the American mainland until the mid-1950s.

- The USA responded by stockpiling thousands of nuclear weapons in Europe and developing **Polaris** submarines, which could fire nuclear weapons (**Submarine-Launched Ballistic Missiles** – SLBMs).

- In the late 1950s and through the 1960s both sides developed ICBMs (**Intercontinental Ballistic Missiles**). By the 1970s Russia had overtaken America in ICBMs and SLBMs. These policies of the two superpowers became known as '**Mutual Assured Destruction**' (MAD).

- By the 1970s the huge amount of money both sides were spending was causing them both problems. In America it led to massive inflation. In Russia it led to lower and lower standards of living and a shortage of consumer goods. Eventually both countries realised the arms race was a pointless waste of money.

Détente continued in the 1970s and 1980s

AQA B
EDEXCEL A
NICCEA

In 1969 Nixon became President of the USA and **Brezhnev** had emerged as leader of the Russian government. Nixon was also desperate to get out of Vietnam and needed to be sure that Russia would stop supporting North Vietnam. Brezhnev announced the '**Brezhnev Doctrine**', in which he welcomed closer links with the West but did not welcome the West criticising what was happening inside Russia.

In 1969 the **Strategic Arms Limitation Talks** (SALT) began. In 1972 **SALT I** was signed. The two countries agreed to limit some types of missiles and to hold more talks about limiting others.

Links between America and Russia grew.

1972	Brezhnev agreed to artistic and sporting links with the USA.
1975	American and Soviet astronauts docked their spacecraft together.
1975	The Helsinki Conference: 35 countries, including America and Russia, reached agreement on a number of matters, e.g. they would tell each other when they were going to hold military manoeuvres; Soviet influence in Eastern Europe was recognised; and Russia agreed to sell oil to the West.

The process of détente slows down

AQA B
EDEXCEL A
NICCEA

In 1977 **Jimmy Carter** became US President. He criticised human rights violations in Russia. In 1979, when Russia invaded Afghanistan, he called on athletes to boycott the Olympic Games in Moscow in 1980 and refused to sign **SALT II.**

Détente was slowing down. It suffered a further blow when **Ronald Reagan** became President of the USA in 1981. Reagan was determined to stand up to Russia and increased spending on arms as well as developing the **Strategic Defence Initiative** (Star Wars), a system designed to destroy any missiles aimed at the USA.

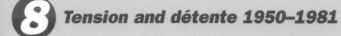
Sample GCSE questions

1. Study Sources A and B and then answer the following questions.

   Source A: The building of the Berlin Wall.

   The frontiers of our country will be protected at any cost. We will do everything to stop the criminal activity of the head-hunters, the slave traders of Western Germany and the American spies.

   From a speech by the Prime Minister of East Germany, 10 August 1961. This speech was made three days before the building of the Berlin Wall was started.

   Source B:

   The Missile Threat 1962.

   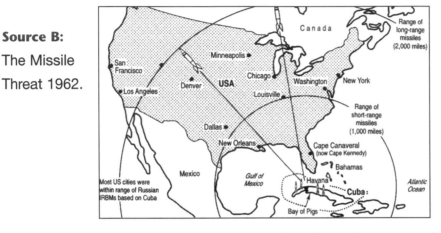

   (a) How reliable is Source A to a historian writing about the reasons for the building of the Berlin Wall? Use Source A and your own knowledge to answer the question. **(6)**

   Source A is not very reliable because it was spoken by the Prime Minister of East Germany and he is obviously trying to justify the building of the Berlin Wall which he knows is just about to happen. The communists built the Wall because lots of skilled workers and scientists in East Berlin were fleeing to West Berlin and they could not afford to lose any more of them. The source does refer to this by talking about `criminal head-hunters´. But the real reason people were going to West Berlin was that the standard of living was better and there was more freedom. The East Germans knew that the only way to keep people in the East was by force – by building a wall. Source A therefore cannot be believed.

   > This answer first discusses who the source was spoken by and what his possible purpose was. Full marks are gained because the answer then goes on to use knowledge to test the reliability of what the East German Prime Minister is saying.

   (b) What can you learn from Source B about the dangers of missiles on Cuba to the USA? **(3)**

   Source B shows that the US was within range of the missiles on Cuba. It shows that nearly all the major cities could be reached by the missiles. This was because Cuba was close to America.

   > Only three marks for this question so there is no need to write a lot. All that is required are three relevant points that can be found in the source.

Sample GCSE questions

(c) Describe how President Kennedy was able to obtain the withdrawal of the Russian missiles from Cuba. **(6)**

Kennedy was able to get the missiles out of Cuba for several reasons. First his idea of a blockade of Cuba was a clever one. It let him stop more missiles coming to Cuba by searching Soviet ships without putting Khrushchev in a position where he had to respond with force. It allowed the Russians to back down without looking too weak. Kennedy was also clever in replying to Khrushchev's first letter where all he asked for was a promise that America would not attack Cuba. In his second letter Khrushchev made more demands - American missiles in Turkey to be removed. Kennedy may have secretly agreed to this.

> *It is important to cover several reasons why Kennedy was able to get the missiles out of Cuba. This answer does this.*

(d) Did relations between the USSR and USA improve between 1955, when Khrushchev came to power, and the setting up of the 'hotline' in 1963? **(10)**

There were ways in which relations between the USSR and the USA improved in this period. This improvement was made possible by the death of Stalin in 1953. Stalin had a very hard line towards the USA and would not compromise. Khrushchev wanted to have peaceful co-existence with the USA and was prepared to sit down and talk about problems with the American President. There was also a new American President - Eisenhower - who was less anti-communist that Truman had been. These changes made better relations possible. The ending of the war in Korea was another factor that helped. Better relations can be seen by the fact that in 1955 Khrushchev and Eisenhower met at the Geneva Conference and agreed to relax Cold War tensions and to start cultural exchanges. The telephone hotline set up after the Cuban crisis was another sign of better relationships.

However, there are ways in which the relationship got worse. The building of the Berlin Wall in 1961 is an example. Khrushchev wanted the West out of Berlin. He hated having this listening post for the West in the middle of East Germany. Several times he demanded that the West leave Berlin but was ignored. The building of the wall increased tension. Tension was also made worse by Russia putting missiles into Cuba, thus threatening America - this could have led to a nuclear war. There was also the shooting down of the American U-2 spy plane over Russia in 1960. This led to a summit meeting between Russia and the USA being cancelled.

Overall, although there were crises, relations between the two countries did improve. At least they started talking to each other through summit meetings and hotlines. When Stalin and Truman were alive this did not happen.

> *This answer provides examples of ways in which relations improved and ways in which relations got worse. Always try and avoid writing a one-sided answer. The next important element of this answer is that it explains several reasons why relations got better and got worse. Finally, it has a conclusion that gives a clear judgement on the question and provides support for that judgement.*

AQA Specimen Paper 1

The collapse of communism

The following topics are covered in this chapter:

- Opposition to Soviet control
- Poland and 'Solidarity' 1980-1989
- Gorbachev and the collapse of communism

9.1 Opposition to Soviet control

LEARNING SUMMARY

After studying this section you will know:

- what happened in Hungary in 1956
- what the consequences of the Hungarian uprising were
- the causes of opposition in Czechoslovakia in 1968
- the results of the 'Prague Spring'
- the similarities and differences between Hungary and Czechoslovakia

Reasons for opposition to Soviet control in Hungary 1956

AQA B
EDEXCEL A
OCR B
NICCEA

As you saw in Chapter 6 the USSR gained control over most of the countries in Eastern Europe soon after the end of the Second World War. These countries had communist governments which were tightly controlled from Moscow. Opponents to communism were dealt with harshly and even communists who did not agree completely with Stalin were imprisoned. The standard of living in the Eastern Bloc was much lower than in the West. Consumer goods that were taken for granted in Western Europe were absent in the East. In 1956 opposition to Soviet control was opposed in Hungary.

The causes of this opposition were as follows:

- Stalin died in 1953. He had kept firm control over Eastern Europe and had immediately stamped on any sign of opposition. His death brought about uncertainty. Would Russia continue to exert the same brutal control?

For Yugoslavia
see page 85.

- Stalin was succeeded by Khrushchev. In 1956 Khrushchev made a speech criticising the way Stalin had ruled Russia and controlled Eastern Europe. He rejected Stalin's brutal methods and said that Russia could live peacefully with the West. He also improved relations with the independent communist state of Yugoslavia and assured Yugoslavs that he believed in non-interference and national independence. This led people in other countries in Eastern Europe, such as Hungary, to expect greater independence.

> **KEY POINT**
>
> In his speech of 1956 Khrushchev gave a misleading impression. He had no intention of letting Eastern European countries be independent of Soviet control.

- In 1956 there were demonstrations in Poland. Although Khrushchev sent in Soviet troops, he also introduced reforms which gave the Poles more freedom. To the people of Hungary this appeared to be another promising sign.

For the Truman Doctrine see page 85.

- The USA sent continuous anti-communist propaganda to Eastern Europe (e.g. by radio). This gave people in Hungary the impression that America would help them if they challenged Soviet control. The Truman Doctrine had promised to help people fighting against communism.

- There was much for Hungarians to oppose. Matyas Rakosi ruled the country with an iron fist: the secret police terrorised any opponents, there was strict censorship and no freedom of speech. The regime was very unpopular.

Examiner's tip: Be ready to explain reasons inside and outside Hungary for the Hungarian revolt.

- In 1956 Rakosi was replaced by Erno Gero. In October a state funeral was held for Laszlo Rajik who had opposed Soviet rule and had been executed. The funeral gave the Hungarians an opportunity to show their opposition to Soviet control. Thousands attended and demonstrations and rioting followed.

What happened in Hungary in 1956

AQA B
EDEXCEL A
OCR B
NICCEA

Fig. 9.1 A wrecked statue of Stalin in Budapest.

1. The demonstrators wanted Imre Nagy to replace Gero. On 24 October Khrushchev agreed to this.
2. This did not end the disturbances. The demonstrators now demanded a free press, an end to one-party rule, the withdrawal of Soviet forces, and Hungary to leave the Warsaw Pact. Nagy agreed to these demands.
3. This was too much for Khrushchev and on 4 November he sent in 200,000 Soviet troops and 2,500 tanks.
4. The Hungarians fought the invading forces and Nagy asked the UN and the West for help. They did nothing.
5. After two weeks of fierce fighting and the deaths of thousands of Hungarians the Soviet forces crushed the resistance.
6. Nagy was replaced by a pro-Soviet government. Nagy was later executed in Russia.

The reaction of Khrushchev

- Khrushchev was happy to accept some reforms in Hungary but he thought the Hungarians' demands went too far. He would not let Hungary leave the Warsaw Pact since this might lead to other countries wanting to leave. This would destroy the protective barrier that had been built to defend the Soviet Union from an attack from the West.

- He acted harshly to set an example to the other Eastern European countries. He wanted to make sure they did not follow Hungary's example.

Results of the Hungarian uprising

For the policy of containment see page 90.

1. A hard-line communist government was established in Hungary.
2. Many Hungarians lost faith in the West. They realised the USA was not going to help them. This was due to the USA's policy of containment of communism.
3. The UN was discredited because it did nothing while Hungary was being invaded.

Reasons for opposition in Czechoslovakia 1968

AQA B
EDEXCEL A
OCR B
NICCEA

The next major opposition to Soviet control in Eastern Europe came in Czechoslovakia.

The Prague Spring – the causes

- Czechoslovakia was a Stalinist state. There was no freedom of speech, heavy censorship and only the Communist Party was allowed to put up candidates in elections. Unrest about all these issues was gradually growing.
- The standard of living for most people was very poor and there were few consumer goods. Economic factors were probably more important than they were in the Hungarian uprising. The Czechs disliked the way their industries were controlled by Russia and run for Russia's benefit.
- In 1968 Alexander Dubcek became the new leader. He was determined to raise living standards and to give people more freedom. He introduced reforms which became known as 'socialism with a human face'. The spring of 1968 became known as the Prague Spring because of the following reforms:

1. government control of industry was reduced, giving more control to managers and workers
2. trades unions were given more freedom
3. censorship of the press was abolished and freedom of expression was allowed
4. criticising the government was no longer a crime
5. it would be easier for Czechs to travel abroad

The reaction of the Soviet Union

Dubcek was a communist and wanted to keep a reformed type of communism. He wanted to keep Czechoslovakia in the Warsaw Pact. He tried to reassure Brezhnev (who had replaced Khrushchev as Soviet leader) that his reforms were no threat to the Soviet Union. However, Brezhnev was not convinced. He could not accept Dubcek's reforms because he feared that:

- freedom of speech would lead to chaos in Czechoslovakia
- the reforms were the first steps to Czechoslovakia becoming a democracy
- Czechoslovakia would leave the Warsaw Pact and join the West – this was dangerous because Czechoslovakia was the link between West Germany and Russia: it could provide a route for American troops to Russia
- if he allowed the reforms other Eastern Bloc countries might want similar reforms: this could lead to the collapse of communism in Eastern Europe
- Dubcek would form an alliance with the independent Yugoslavia and with Romania, another communist country that resented Soviet control

Fig. 9.2 A Czechoslovakian cartoon from 1968 commenting on the Soviet reaction to the Prague Spring.

Brezhnev ordered troops and tanks to the Czech border. Dubcek responded by inviting the leaders of Yugoslavia and Romania to a meeting. On 20 August 1968 the Russian forces, with forces from East Germany, Poland and Bulgaria, invaded Czechoslovakia.

The Czech Government decided not to resist the invading forces. Although there was some street fighting the casualty figures of the Hungarian rising were not repeated. In 1969 Dubcek was removed from office. Thousands of Czechs were arrested. Czechoslovakia was once more under Soviet control.

Examiner's tip:
Make sure you have noted the similarities and the differences between events in Hungary and Czechoslovakia.

Results of the Prague Spring

1. The Brezhnev Doctrine. Brezhnev stated that Russia was not prepared to allow any country in Eastern Europe to abandon communism. If they tried, Russia would stop them.
2. Communists were disillusioned by the actions of the Soviet Union. They began looking for a new type of communism.
3. A hard-line communist government was set up.

Comparing Hungary 1956 with Czechoslovakia 1968

AQA B
EDEXCEL A
OCR B
NICCEA

Similarities

The similarities are clear:

- opposition to Soviet control
- reforms passed that the Soviet Union did not like
- the Russian army being used to suppress opposition

From Russia's point of view the two events were very similar: they both threatened the safety of the Soviet Union. However, the differences are just as important.

Differences

- Hungary wanted to leave the Warsaw Pact; Czechoslovakia did not.
- Economic factors were more important in Czechoslovakia.
- The Hungarians put up much more resistance to the Soviet invasion and many more people were killed.
- The Soviet reaction was less extreme in Czechoslovakia. Dubcek was not executed.

PROGRESS CHECK

1. Give four reasons why opposition to Soviet control appeared in Hungary.
2. Write down four main events of the Hungarian uprising in the order in which they happened.
3. Give three reasons why Brezhnev was worried about events in Czechoslovakia in 1968.
4. Give two ways in which events in Hungary and Czechoslovakia were similar and two ways in which they were different.

1. The death of Stalin; Khrushchev's rejection of Stalin's methods; introduction of reforms by Khrushchev; support from America. 2. Nagy replaced by Gero; demonstrations for more freedom and Hungary to leave Warsaw Pact; Soviet troops invade and the Hungarians were defeated; Nagy replaced. 3. Dubcek's reforms would lead to chaos with Czechoslovakia leaving the Warsaw Pact; other countries might follow; danger of alliance between Czechoslovakia, Yugoslavia and Romania. 4. Similarities: opposition to Soviet control; Soviet army used to put down opposition. Differences: Hungary wanted to leave the Warsaw Pact, Czechoslovakia did not; Soviet reaction more extreme in Hungary.

9.2 Poland and 'Solidarity' 1980–1989

LEARNING SUMMARY

After studying this section you will know:

- why opposition to Soviet control appeared in Poland
- the main events in Poland from 1980–1989
- the reasons for Solidarity's success

Reasons for opposition to Soviet control in Poland

AQA B
OCR B
NICCEA

Fig. 9.3 Lech Walesa.

The next country to grow restless with Soviet control was Poland. There are several reasons why Poland was to cause much trouble for the Soviet Union.

- The Poles had long hated the Russians. Much of Poland had been governed by Russia for hundreds of years.

- Many Poles were Catholic. The communist regime did not approve of the Catholic Church, but it was too strong to be destroyed and acted as a focus for opposition to communism.

- The Poles had a tradition of protesting and striking against the government. There had been protests in Poland in 1949, 1956 and 1970. Each time the government was forced to make changes.

- During the 1970s Poland was more prosperous than other communist countries in Eastern Europe. By 1980 this had changed. The standard of living fell sharply while prices of food, fuel and clothing rose. Workers formed trades unions and went on strike.

- The most important of these trades unions was Solidarity, a union of the workers at the Gdansk shipyards. It was led by Lech Walesa. His leadership was crucial. He was a brilliant speaker and Solidarity soon had 9 million members.

- Solidarity at first demanded better wages and working conditions but was soon making political demands: democratic elections with parties other than the Communist Party allowed to stand.
- Russia considered sending in troops but did not because Solidarity and Walesa were too popular.

The main events in Poland 1980–1989

AQA B
OCR B
NICCEA

1. The Soviet Union appointed a new leader of the Polish Government – General Jaruzelski. He was told he had to deal with Solidarity or there would be a Soviet invasion.

2. In December 1981 Jaruzelski imposed military law, banned Solidarity, and arrested Walesa and thousands of supporters of Solidarity. Soviet troops massed on the Polish border.

3. Jaruzelski tried to set up a union to replace Solidarity but Poles were not interested. Walesa was now a national and international hero. In 1982 he was released from prison and in 1983 awarded the Nobel Peace Prize.

4. Jaruzelski was losing his authority. In 1986 Solidarity stopped price rises by threatening to call a general strike.

5. In 1989 Jaruzelski was forced to hold free elections. Solidarity won a massive victory. Jaruzelski tried to hang on to power but soon Solidarity was in charge of the government. Poland had a non-communist government with Walesa as president.

Reasons why Solidarity succeeded

> **Jaruzelski was under pressure from Russia to deal with Solidarity but he then found Gorbachev undermining him by passing reforms.**

- Solidarity had such massive support in Poland that it was impossible for the Soviet Union simply to destroy it.
- Solidarity did not attempt to fight an armed battle with the Soviets as the Hungarians had. Solidarity used strikes, which were much more difficult to deal with.
- At this time Mikhail Gorbachev, leader of Russia, was introducing reforms in the Soviet Union, giving people more freedom. This encouraged the people of Poland and made the hard line adopted by Jaruzelski harder to maintain.

PROGRESS CHECK

1. Name four reasons why there was opposition to Soviet control in Poland.
2. Name the general who was appointed leader of the Polish Government.
3. Give three reasons why Solidarity was successful.
4. Name the leader of Solidarity.

1. Poles traditionally hated the Russians; influence of the Catholic Church; fall in living standards; the actions of Solidarity. 2. General Jaruzelski. 3. It was very popular; it used strikes instead of an armed uprising; Gorbachev's reforms in Russia. 4. Lech Walesa.

9.3 Gorbachev and the collapse of communism

LEARNING SUMMARY

After studying this section you will know:

- why Gorbachev began to reform the Soviet Union
- what these reforms were
- how communism collapsed in Eastern Europe

Why Gorbachev introduced reforms into the Soviet Union

AQA B
EDEXCEL A
OCR B
NICCEA

Poland was not the only country to break away from communism in 1989. To find the reasons for these changes we need to look at what was happening in Russia. In 1985 Gorbachev became leader of the Soviet Union. He realised that reforms were badly needed. Russia was facing many problems and communism was making things worse.

- Living standards were poor.
- There was much corruption, with Communist Party bosses living in luxury.
- Russian farming was very inefficient. Russia was having to import grain.
- Russian industry was out of date and could not keep up with the West in new areas such as computers.
- The Soviet Union was spending a huge proportion of its national income on weapons because of the Cold War. In 1979 Russia had invaded Afghanistan. This war was costing $8 billion a year.

> Gorbachev was forced to pass reforms because of the dire economic state of Russia. It could not pay for its expensive foreign policy and could not give its own people a decent standard of living.

Gorbachev's reforms

Gorbachev planned to introduce '**perestroika**' (restructuring the economy to make it more efficient) and '**glasnost**' (openness to new ideas and more free speech).

Reforms in Russia

- Political prisoners were released.
- Farmers were allowed to farm for private profit.
- Managers in industry were given more freedom.

However, there was much opposition to these reforms and living standards fell. Russia was in danger of falling into chaos.

Foreign policy

- In 1987 Gorbachev signed a disarmament treaty with America.
- In 1988 he announced that the Brezhnev Doctrine was abandoned. Russia would not interfere in Eastern Europe.
- Cuts in Soviet armed forces were announced.
- In 1989 Gorbachev withdrew troops from Afghanistan.

By 1989 it was clear that the Soviet Union was not able and not prepared to hold its empire together, nor to maintain its control over Eastern Europe.

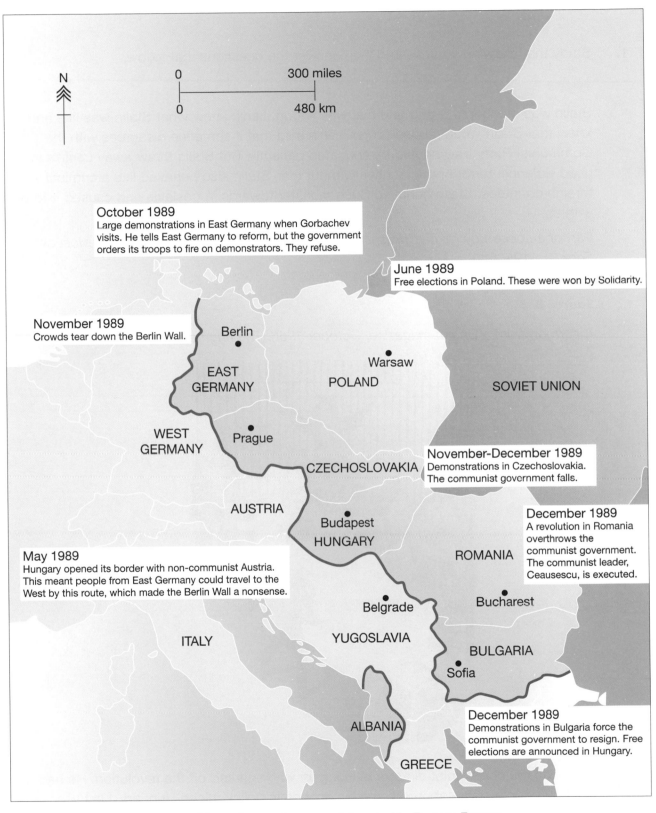

October 1989
Large demonstrations in East Germany when Gorbachev visits. He tells East Germany to reform, but the government orders its troops to fire on demonstrators. They refuse.

June 1989
Free elections in Poland. These were won by Solidarity.

November 1989
Crowds tear down the Berlin Wall.

Berlin

Warsaw

EAST GERMANY

POLAND

SOVIET UNION

WEST GERMANY

Prague

November–December 1989
Demonstrations in Czechoslovakia. The communist government falls.

CZECHOSLOVAKIA

AUSTRIA

Budapest

HUNGARY

December 1989
A revolution in Romania overthrows the communist government. The communist leader, Ceausescu, is executed.

ROMANIA

May 1989
Hungary opened its border with non-communist Austria. This meant people from East Germany could travel to the West by this route, which made the Berlin Wall a nonsense.

Belgrade

Bucharest

ITALY

YUGOSLAVIA

BULGARIA

Sofia

December 1989
Demonstrations in Bulgaria force the communist government to resign. Free elections are announced in Hungary.

ALBANIA

GREECE

N

0   300 miles
0   480 km

Fig. 9.4 The collapse of communist control in Eastern Europe.

Communism in Eastern Europe had simply collapsed. In 1990 the two halves of Germany were united. In 1991 the republics that made up the USSR declared their independence. The Soviet Union was no more.

Exam practice questions

1. Study the following sources and then answer the questions that follow.

Source A

Stalin was made into a god and that was wrong. Lenin knew what Stalin was like and he knew that Stalin would abuse power. Lenin said that if someone disagrees with the Communist Party they should be educated patiently. But Stalin threw away Lenin's ideas and used violence, terror and execution without trial. Stalin also behaved like a criminal with foreign countries. Stalin behaved like a monster towards Yugoslavia and caused it to break with us.

Part of a speech by Nikita Khrushchev to the Communist Party Conference, Moscow, February 1956.

Source B

A cartoon from a British magazine, October 1956. The ringmaster is Nikita Khrushchev.

Source C

Gero was the communist dictator of Hungary who sparked off the revolution. He had made 120,000 people slave-labourers and his economic policy ruined Hungary. Last year he smiled for only the second time in his life when, at 9 p.m. on 23 October, he ordered the Hungarian Secret Police to machine-gun students outside Budapest radio station.

A Hungarian historian who took part in the revolution, writing in a British newspaper, 7 April 1957.

Exam practice questions

1.

(a) Study Source A. Why did this speech give hope to people in countries controlled by the Soviet Union? Explain your answer, using details of the speech and your own knowledge. **(6)**

....

....

....

....

....

(b) Study Source B. What point is the cartoonist making about the Soviet Union's control of Eastern Europe in 1956? Explain your answer, using details of the cartoon and your own knowledge. **(8)**

....

....

....

....

....

....

....

....

(c) Study Source C. Do you believe this explanation of the causes of the revolution in Hungary in 1956? Explain your answer, using details of the source and your own knowledge. **(8)**

....

....

....

....

....

....

....

....

OCR Paper 2, 2000

Chapter 10

Britain 1919–1951

The following topics are covered in this chapter:

- *1919–1929: the General Strike*
- *1929–1939: depression and recovery*
- *1939–1951: a changed society?*

10.1 1919–1929: the General Strike

LEARNING SUMMARY

After studying this section you will know:

- *how Britain recovered very slowly from the First World War*
- *why the problems of declining industries seemed insoluble*
- *the reasons for the General Strike*
- *the roles of the government and the Trade Union Congress in ending the strike*

Britain's industries in decline after the First World War

AQA B

In the Coupon Election, in December 1918, **Lloyd George was triumphantly returned at the head of a coalition government**, mostly made up of Conservatives. They enjoyed a short post-war boom in industry, and by late 1919 over 4 million troops were 'demobbed'.

Inflation and strikes

At the end of the war there was sudden inflation; **prices rose uncontrollably, but wages lagged behind**. Trades unions were determined to protect their workers, and between 1919 and 1920 there were **over 2,000 strikes**. Disillusionment from the trenches and the success of Bolshevism in Russia helped to inflame the situation.

- There was a serious strike **of Clydeside engineers and shipbuilders** in 1919. This resulted in the calling in of troops and tanks.

- The **Miners' Federation** demanded a six-hour day, a 30 per cent wage increase and continued government control of the mines. Lloyd George offered a seven-hour day and continued government control, but appointed the **Sankey Commission** to investigate the problem.

Slump 1921

- **The slow decline of British industry since the 1870s** (which had been temporarily reversed with war production) became evident again. Industrialists were losing the race towards greater mechanisation and investment in industry.

- **Foreign buyers**, unable to get British goods during the war, **had found alternative suppliers**. So demand for traditional British exports (ships, textiles, iron, steel, coal) never reached pre-war levels.
- The government increased aid to the unemployed (the 'dole') but did not attack the root of the problem – industry's declining profitability.
- The Sankey Commission could not find a solution to the mining problems. The whole industry came out on strike but the mines and railways were put back into private ownership on 1 April.
- Miners' wages were reduced because of the drop in exports.
- **The miners were then forced to take wage reductions, as were workers in the engineering, docks, shipbuilding, textiles, printing and railway industries.**
- Lloyd George lost popularity among the workers and therefore lost the election in October 1922.
- **By the end of 1921 there were 2 million unemployed in Britain**. The figure would never fall below 1 million again until 1939.

> The miners could not make the strike general because they were betrayed by their allies in the railway and transport industries. However, they continued to strike for three months.

The failure of the first Labour Government

After a short-lived Conservative government, **Ramsay MacDonald headed the first Labour Government in January 1924**. It failed to solve industrial problems because:

- it could not afford to be too radical as it relied on Liberal votes to stay in office
- it was seen as biased towards trades union interests (but the unions thought it was too independent of their wishes)
- Labour had no answers to the industrial problems beyond nationalisation, which was impractical

The Labour Government fell in October 1924. Stanley Baldwin and the Conservatives took power, with a huge majority of 200 MPs.

The General Strike

AQA B

The background to the strike

- There was continuing post-war depression.
- Decline of important industries continued.
- Liberal and Labour attempts to solve the problems of the mining industry failed.
- Falling exports and mass unemployment also had an effect.

Causes

- In April 1925 **Winston Churchill**, Conservative Chancellor of the Exchequer, **took Britain back onto the gold standard**. Economists have estimated that he over-valued the pound sterling by about 10 per cent.

By taking Britain back onto the gold standard, Churchill pegged the pound sterling to an absolute value in gold. While producing a sound, reliable currency it over-valued the pound against foreign currencies. So British wages seemed high compared to those abroad, and British export prices were also too high.

> Germany and Poland could sell cheap coal partly because their mines were mechanised. Only 20 per cent of British mines used machines; most miners still used hand picks.

- British mining was worse hit than any other industry because in June 1925 **cheap German coal** from the Ruhr became available at a time when competition was growing from gas, electricity and oil industries.

In June 1925, **mine owners announced that they would have to reduce wages and increase hours** to be able to sell coal at an economic price. The miners protested. Prime Minister Stanley Baldwin saved the situation by appointing the **Samuel Commission** to find a solution.

> Examiner's tip: Make sure you know the *causes* of the strike.

- The **Trades Union Congress (TUC) said it would support the miners** because a reduction in their wages would signal a further reduction in wages throughout industry.

- The **Samuel Commission reported** in April 1926. It recommended:

  1. that mine owners should press ahead with modernisation
  2. the government should withdraw its subsidy
  3. that miners should accept a temporary reduction in their wages (to be restored when the crisis was over)

Neither the owners nor the miners accepted the report. The government did not force them, and the TUC tried to keep negotiations going because it could not afford a General Strike.

Fig. 10.1 One view of the issues at stake. A cartoon from *Punch* (19 May 1926).

- The mine owners announced that wages would be reduced from 30 April. **The miners** decided to strike on 1 May, but they were **locked out by the mine owners on 30 April**. The TUC announced that a General Strike would begin on 3 May if a settlement had not been reached.

- Last-minute negotiations between the TUC and the Cabinet on 2 May were hampered when the miners' leaders went home. *Daily Mail* compositors refused to print an article branding the strike as revolutionary. **Baldwin was furious** and **ended the talks**. The TUC went to Downing Street to protest, but found the Cabinet had gone home and Baldwin was in bed.

The strike

The response to the strike was almost 100 per cent in the industries called out by the TUC (road, rail, docks, printing, gas and electricity, building, iron, steel and chemicals).

By 11 May there was no sign of a climbdown on either side. **Sir Herbert Samuel** offered to mediate. The TUC accepted.

The **Samuel Memorandum** suggested:

1. a short-term renewal of the subsidy to allow wages to be maintained during the reorganisation of the mining industry
2. a National Wages Board

On 12 May the TUC **called off the General Strike**, hoping the Memorandum would be accepted. Baldwin had given no guarantees.

- There was no sign of the government giving ground.
- The TUC was completely unprepared for a General Strike and was scared it would escalate.
- In the House of Commons Sir John Simon (a Liberal lawyer) had said that the strike was not an industrial dispute but an 'illegal proceeding' and strike leaders could therefore be sued or gaoled.
- The TUC had already used £4 million of its £12 million strike fund.

The strike lasted unofficially until 14 May. Even then the miners refused to return to work. The mine owners would not compromise and the strike dragged on until December. The miners were forced to accept lower wages and longer hours, and were bitter at their 'betrayal' by the TUC.

How well did Baldwin handle the strike?

> Churchill had suggested using armoured cars to protect convoys and used phrases such as 'We are at war'.

Well	Badly
• Baldwin *played a waiting game*, knowing the TUC could not hold out for long.	• He allowed right-wingers (Churchill) to be aggressive in the British Gazette.
• Baldwin saw the strike as an attack on the Constitution, so no negotiations could begin until it ended.	• King George V had to tell Baldwin to restrain Churchill.
• The government had prepared months ahead. Volunteers kept food supplies moving, protected convoys etc.	
• Baldwin was conciliatory in tone when he appealed to the nation on 8 May, asking for a fair deal for everyone.	

The results of the strike

- The working class was disillusioned with the TUC. Its membership slumped from over 8 million in 1926 to under 5 million in 1927.
- There was no solution to the problems of the coal industry, which continued to decline. In 1913 it exported 73 million tons; in 1932 39 million tons.
- The strike showed reasonable employers that wage reductions were not an easy solution to their difficulties.
- The TUC realised a General Strike would never succeed. The working class turned to parliamentary action. This was partly responsible for the increase in Labour Party support in the 1929 general election.

● The government introduced the **Trades Disputes Act 1927**. This made sympathetic strikes and intimidation illegal and stopped trade unions from automatically contributing towards the Labour Party from members' subscriptions.

PROGRESS CHECK

1. What commission was appointed by Lloyd George to look into the problems in the mining industry?
2. How did Winston Churchill make the economic situation worse in 1925?
3. What did the Samuel Commission recommend to the government in April 1926?

1. The Sankey Commission. 2. He returned Britain to the gold standard. 3. That mine owners should press ahead with modernisation; that the government should withdraw its subsidy; that miners should accept a temporary reduction in their wages (to be restored when the crisis was over).

10.2 1929–1939: depression and recovery

LEARNING SUMMARY

After studying this section you will know:

● *how the Wall Street Crash affected Britain*
● *why the Labour government was unable to deal with the country's economic problems*
● *how uneven the effects of the Depression were in the north and south*
● *why some people became better off while wages were reduced*

The Wall Street Crash and the onset of the Depression made an already difficult situation in Europe worse.

The effects of the Wall Street Crash on Europe

AQA B
EDEXCEL A
WJEC A   WJEC B

European prosperity was bound up with its ability to repay America, especially the Dawes Plan of 1924. German loans were used to pay reparations to Britain, France, Belgium and Italy, who then repaid their war debts to the USA.

Even before the Wall Street Crash, American overproduction and protective tariffs were reducing Europe's ability to repay US loans.
But in 1929 the USA:

● ceased to import goods from Europe
● stopped all future loans to Germany
● called in all short-term loans to Germany

Germany was hit most severely. Britain, one of Germany's main creditors and trading partners, was also badly affected.

The Labour Government 1929–1931

The second Labour Government had taken power under **Ramsay MacDonald** after the general election of 1929. Unemployment increased from 1 million to 2.5 million by December 1930, yet it took no action to reduce it. Solutions suggested by radicals such as Sir Oswald Moseley and Lloyd George were ignored. Increasing unemployment was leading to financial crisis, so the government appointed Sir George May to investigate national expenditure.

Sir George May's committee took until July 1931 to report. It proposed:

- a general reduction of salaries in the public sector (armed forces, civil servants, judges and police)
- teachers were singled out for cuts of 20 per cent

The result was a sudden loss of confidence. Foreign investors thought Britain must be bankrupt and withdrew their investments. Further reductions in government expenditure were demanded to restore confidence.

MacDonald and his Chancellor, Snowden, were prepared to go ahead with the May Committee proposals but ten out of 21 members of the Cabinet refused to agree to any cut in unemployment benefit.

MacDonald was forced to resign. He emerged as leader of a coalition National Government. It consisted mostly of Conservatives and Liberals with only three Labour members.

The National Government 1931–1935

AQA B
EDEXCEL A
WJEC A   WJEC B

Emergency measures were implemented in Snowden's budget on the lines of the May Report:

- **income tax was raised** from 4s 6d to 5s in the pound
- **salaries of public employees were reduced by 10 per cent**

This did not restore confidence. In September 1931 naval crews protested against salary cuts in the **Invergordon Mutiny.** This was only settled when the government promised not to cut further.

A 'Doctor's mandate' meant that the country should trust the Prime Minister as if he were a doctor, without knowing the reasons behind his actions.

- The government took the pound off the gold standard. Its value was allowed to fall by about 25 per cent; there was still no revival in exports. Unemployment continued to rise towards 3 million.

- Ramsay MacDonald called a surprise general election in October. He asked for a 'doctor's mandate' and won a majority with 521 MPs from different parties.

- In 1932 free trade was finally abandoned by Neville Chamberlain's **Import Duties Act**. This placed a 10 per cent duty on most imports, except those from the Empire.

- Defence expenditure and interest on war loans were reduced.

Many local authorities took the opportunity to build council houses, helping to relieve local unemployment.

- Attempts were made to rationalise and modernise the iron, steel, coal, textiles and shipbuilding industries.

- The bank rate was reduced from 6 per cent to 2 per cent to reduce debt charges.

- **The Unemployment Act 1934** set up the National Unemployment Assistance Board, with branches all over the country. It paid out benefit after an unemployed man ran out of the normal period of insurance benefit. It caused great bitterness because it was based on a **means test** introduced in 1931. This took into account the total family income and savings before paying out dole money. It therefore penalised the thrifty.

- **The Special Areas Act 1934** provided £2 million to revive the depressed areas.

Gradual Recovery, 1932–1939

Some measure of prosperity may have returned without the measures outlined above for a number of reasons.

- **Prices had fallen faster than wages.** The world was suffering from oversupply so there was an increase in real wages.

- **People were able to spend their extra cash on British consumer goods and even luxuries**, which stimulated the economy. Unemployment had fallen to 2 million by 1935 and 1.4 million by 1937 (though there was an increase in 1938).

BUT

- Some areas (e.g. the Midlands and the South) did well because of increased population and modern industries (e.g. automobile, aeronautical and electrical). Others (e.g. Scotland, the North-East, Cumberland, Lancashire and Northern Ireland) did very badly because they were dependent on declining basic industries (e.g. coal, iron, steel, shipbuilding and textiles).

- In 1934 Jarrow had 68 per cent unemployment, Merthyr Tydfil 62 per cent and St Albans only 3.9 per cent.

- In Stockton-on-Tees the average income of families where the wage-earner was unemployed was only £1 10s a week.

- The average infant mortality rate in the South was 42 per thousand live births; in South Wales it was 63, in Durham and Northumberland 76 and in Jarrow 114.

PROGRESS CHECK

1. Why did Ramsay MacDonald's first Labour Government fall in 1931?
2. Which measure, which helped to restore the economy, was taken as the immediate result of the Invergordon Mutiny?
3. Why did people seem better off by 1939, when wages were reduced in 1932?

1. Because they agreed with the recommendations of Sir George May's committee to reduce public sector salaries. Creditors thought the government was bankrupt and the Cabinet split and refused to implement the proposals. 2. Britain abandoned the gold standard. 3. Because world prices were falling faster than wages.

10.3 1939–1951: a changed society?

LEARNING SUMMARY

After studying this section you will know:

- the impact of the Second World War on Britain
- the reasons for far-reaching reforms in the late 1940s
- the details of the creation of the Welfare State

Only the coming of war in 1939 solved the long-term problems of unemployment and deprivation.

The impact of the Second World War

AQA B
EDEXCEL A
WJEC A   WJEC B

The civilian population was directly involved in the war from the beginning through:

- mass evacuation of children from the cities
- digging shelters, piling sandbags, issuing gas masks
- maintaining and enforcing the blackout
- removal of signposts, place names and station name-boards
- rationing of bacon, butter, cheese and meat; later clothes and fuel
- conscription of women as well as men
- volunteering for the Home Guard
- the German bombing, especially of London, Coventry, Liverpool, Manchester, Plymouth, Hull, Glasgow and Belfast
- hundreds of thousands were made homeless

> The bombing killed about 60,000 (half in London) and seriously injured about 100,000.

The war caused **an acceleration of social change**. Many were appalled at the state of evacuee children and impressed by the co-operation of all classes of society in a truly national effort. **The poor, it was felt, had earned concessions**. There was a fear of revolution after the war if concessions were not made quickly. There were two immediate results: the Beveridge Report and the Butler Education Act.

The Beveridge Report 1942

Churchill's National Government appointed a committee, under **Sir William Beveridge**, a Liberal, to investigate the problems of social insurance. The report said that the great evils in society were **want, disease, ignorance, squalor and idleness**. These would be eliminated by government insurance schemes, child allowances, a national health service and a policy of full employment. Churchill did not agree with the report and had only implemented child allowances before the end of his government in 1945.

The Butler Education Act 1944

R.A. Butler, Conservative President of the Board of Education, **made free secondary education available to all**, and raised the school leaving age to 15. Secondary schools were to be either grammar, technical or modern.

The economic cost of the war

Britain was impoverished and her gold reserves exhausted within the first two years of the war. In March 1941 the US Congress passed the **Lend Lease Act**, which allowed Britain to obtain crucial supplies from America, to be paid for later. By 1945 Britain's overseas debts had reached well over £3,000 million. After Japan was defeated President Truman abruptly ended Lend Lease and demanded repayment of the debt. **The only solution was to agree a new loan from the USA on very unfavourable terms, which reduced Britain to dependency.**

The end of Empire

The British Empire was intact in 1945, but within 20 years most colonies had achieved independence. **Nationalist feelings had been stirred by British defeats, especially in India and the Far East. Britain was now only a second-rate power.**

Labour in power 1945–1951

AQA B
EDEXCEL A
WJEC A   WJEC B

In May 1945, the Labour Party under **Clement Attlee** gained a massive victory over the Conservatives, with 393 seats to the Conservatives' 213. While Churchill had remained personally popular, the Conservative majority in the National Government was blamed for appeasement and for failing to implement the Beveridge Report. **The first Labour Government with a real majority was hampered by huge economic problems:**

- the premature ending of Lend Lease
- the loss of two-thirds of Britain's export trade
- the sinking of much of Britain's merchant fleet

However, the Labour Government completed an astonishing list of measures, which created the post-war consensus that survived into the 1970s.

Nationalisation

This was to give the **government control of Britain's most important industries**; permit more efficient planning and co-operation between industries; and ensure fair treatment and better working conditions for employees.

Under the direction of Herbert Morrison (Leader of the House of Commons) the following industries were nationalised:

Nationalisation of iron and steel was delayed by the House of Lords, because these industries were reasonably efficient, but after the passing of the Parliament Act 1949 they were finally nationalised in 1950.

- Bank of England (1946)
- coal industry (1947)
- public transport (1948), including inland waterways, railways, docks, road haulage, road passenger transport and London Transport
- electricity (1948)
- gas (1949)
- iron and steel (1950)

Export or die

> **KEY POINT**
>
> **The balance of payments deficit**
> It is important to have a balance between the cost of goods exported and imported, or that a country should export more than it imports. If imports are too high there is an outflow of wealth from the country. This is the balance of payments deficit.

The aim was **to return exports to their pre-war level** so the balance of payments deficit would be removed. A loan was needed to restore industry to peacetime production levels.

J.M. Keynes, the famous economist, was **sent to the USA to negotiate an interest-free loan of $6,000 million**. The Americans drove a hard bargain. He returned with only $3,750 million dollars, at 2 per cent interest, with repayments starting in 1951. By 1947 it had been almost used up, but industry was recovering and had reached **17 per cent above the 1939 figure for exports**. However, the balance of payments deficit stood at £438 million.

George Marshall, American Secretary of State, was worried about the poor prospects for American trade and the spread of communism in Europe. He **offered grants to any country in Europe that would accept them. Britain took a gift of £1,263 million in Marshall Aid.** This enabled recovery to be completed. By 1950, exports were 75 per cent above the 1938 level.

The Welfare State

AQA B
EDEXCEL A
WJEC A   WJEC B

The Labour Party had been elected on a promise to put the **Beveridge Report** into action. In fact, it had its own plans for a comprehensive social security scheme, family allowances and a national health service.

The National Health Service Act 1946

The architect was **Aneurin Bevan**, Minister of Health, who faced strong opposition from the medical profession. From 1948 the system gave everyone:

- free medical care from their own doctor
- free specialist care and hospital treatment in nationalised hospitals
- free eye tests, eye treatment and spectacles
- free dentistry, false teeth, drugs, midwifery, maternity and child welfare

The scheme was financed partly from taxation and partly from National Insurance contributions. It was expensive. It cost over £400 million in its first year. This led Hugh Gaitskell, Chancellor of the Exchequer, to begin charging adults for half the cost of false teeth and spectacles.

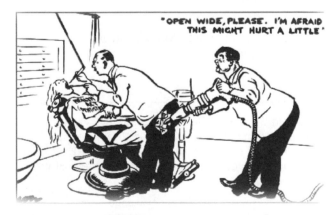

"OPEN WIDE, PLEASE. I'M AFRAID THIS MIGHT HURT A LITTLE"

Fig. 10.2 *Evening Standard*, July 1948.
A humorous view of Bevan's achievement.

Aneurin Bevan resigned, believing the principle of an entirely free health service had been violated.

National Insurance

A compulsory National Insurance scheme was begun in 1946. All workers contributed. The scheme gave contributors sickness and unemployment benefit, old age pensions, widows' and orphans' pensions and maternity and death grants.

In 1948 National Assistance Boards were set up to help those too old to be insured under the new scheme. Social services were to be provided by local authorities for the elderly and handicapped. The National Insurance Industrial Injuries Act 1946 made employers and employees contribute to a state scheme to compensate workers and provide pensions for the disabled.

Education

Under the Butler Education Act of 1944 children took an 11-plus exam to select which secondary school they would attend. Ordinary Levels at 16 and Advanced Levels at 18 replaced the old School Certificate system.

Housing

Houses	
1946	55,400
1947	139,690
1948	284,230

There was already a housing shortage in 1939, but **the war destroyed 700,000 more houses.** Bevan launched a new housing drive. Despite the high cost of building materials considerable numbers were completed, rising to over 200,000 a year before 1951. Although more houses were built than the number expected to be needed, **the increase in marriages and rise in the birth rate after the war meant housing remained in short supply.**

Two other measures helped improve housing.

The New Towns Act 1946

- gave the government the **power to establish new towns**, appoint development corporations and carry out projects
- healthy, pleasant new towns were created at Stevenage, Crawley, Hemel Hempstead and Harlow, East Kilbride, Peterlee and Glenrothes
- 14 new towns were established by the end of the government's time in office

The Town and Country Planning Act 1947

- gave the job of planning to county councils
- they had to plan land development 20 years ahead
- they were given powers of compulsory purchase, could control advertisements and protect historic buildings

PROGRESS CHECK

1. List the five great evils described in Sir William Beveridge's report.
2. Which Conservative minister opened up secondary education to all?
3. Which Labour minister was the architect of the National Health Service?
4. What payments were made by workers to cover the costs of the Welfare State?

1. Want, disease, ignorance, squalor and idleness 2. R.A. Butler 3. Aneurin Bevan 4. National Insurance Contributions.

Sample GCSE questions

1.

(a)   Give two examples of groups taking industrial action in 1919.   **(4)**

Clydeside engineers and shipbuilders; miners.

Keep these short: two marks for each group named.

(b)   Why was there a General Strike in 1926?   **(6)**

High wages and under-investment in the mining industry meant that foreign coal was much cheaper than British coal. In 1926 the German coalfields were exporting cheap coal and the British mining industry decided it needed longer hours and lower wages to compete.

Winston Churchill had just returned the pound to the gold standard, reducing the competitiveness of British exports and allowing imports to undercut our industries.

The mine owners decided to reduce wages because the Samuel Commission had recommended that the government subsidy should be withdrawn. Neither the government nor the miners bothered to keep negotiations going, despite the efforts of the TUC.

Two good reasons are enough here, but explain each in its own short paragraph. The candidate has developed each of these sufficiently and did not need to make three points.

(c)   'It was only the level-headed attitude of Stanley Baldwin that prevented the General Strike from escalating towards real civil unrest.' Do you agree with this statement? Explain your answer. **(10)**

Baldwin did not see the urgency of the situation and actually went to bed rather than continue negotiations with the TUC. This helped to cause the strike. His refusal to negotiate while the strike continued probably prolonged it, and he certainly did not restrain the rest of his Cabinet. The King had to tell Baldwin to control them, especially Winston Churchill, whose British Gazette was inciting the middle classes to confront the strikers. Churchill also called out the army to guard food convoys, when volunteers were doing the job well. Baldwin was not so much level-headed as idle.

The question is quite controversial and needs a 'for and against' answer. The first half here is put quite effectively.

Baldwin had prepared the country some time in advance, and realised the TUC did not have the funds to continue the strike for long. He saw the strike as an attack on the Constitution, but did not take sides himself. He was very conciliatory when he addressed the nation, asking for a fair deal for everyone. The government enforced the law irrespective of the political opinions of its individual members.

The second half of the answer is effectively argued but there is no conclusion. This would help to make the judgement clear.

In any case it is doubtful whether any group intended to push the dispute to the extent of civil war. The TUC had made every effort to settle even before the strike began, and took the first opportunity of calling it off, once Sir Herbert Samuel suggested a compromise.

The following topics are covered in this chapter:

- Russia before the First World War
- The impact of the First World War
- March to November 1917
- Bolshevik victory: November 1917
- Bolshevik rule and its impact 1918–1928
- Stalin's dictatorship

11.1 Russia before the First World War

LEARNING SUMMARY

After studying this section you will know:

- *why Russia was unstable before the First World War*
- *the identity and aims of several important political parties in the Duma*

Russian society before 1914

AQA B
EDEXCEL A
OCR B
WJEC A
NICCEA

Society breaking apart

Serfdom This continued until 1861. It was ended by a compromise which left neither the nobility nor the serfs satisfied. The peasants (freed serfs) suffered a 49 year indemnity (mortgage) on their land, and received less land than they expected.

Illiteracy Only about 30% of peasants were literate by 1914. It had been the policy of the Tsars to keep them ignorant.

Nobility losing influence The aristocracy still had great power in the army, civil service, local government and as landowners. They disliked their loss of authority since the freeing of the serfs. Money compensation was soon spent. They resented the fact that the Nicholas II shut himself and his family away at Tsarskoe Selo (Tsar's Village) outside St Petersburg. They preferred Grand Duke Michael, the Tsar's popular brother.

Middle classes dissatisfied In towns the middle class was small, but growing by 1914. Professional people and industrialists thought that Tsardom ignored their needs and hoped for a constitutional Government.

Poor urban conditions The few industrial towns acted as magnets for the landless peasantry and were growing very fast. This resulted in a poor standard of building, hygiene and public amenities. Moscow and St Petersburg (the capital) were expanding hugely. A growing group of permanent urban workers resented their poor living and working conditions and resorted to strikes and demonstrations to make their protests felt.

KEY POINT

A constitutional government is organised according to a set of rules (a constitution) which regulates the relationships between the ruler and the ruled. It usually implies some kind of democracy.

By 1914 Russian society was breaking apart. Each class followed its own interests and none was very loyal to the Tsar. Society was heading towards a crisis. This was delayed by the patriotism the nation felt when it found itself at war.

The economy before 1914

AQA B
EDEXCEL A
OCR B
WJEC A
NICCEA

Subsistence farming means that they produced what they needed, took little to market, did not use much money and could not easily be taxed.

Russia was a poor country. She had great resources but these were 'locked in' by the vast size of the country and the extreme climate. She had produced cheap raw materials for other manufacturing countries and a growing surplus of grain, but it was the policy of the Tsars from 1855 to compete as a manufacturing power.

- In1914 **85 per cent of the population were still peasants**.
- Peasants had to practise **subsistence farming**.
- Economically, the vast majority of the population contributed very little to Russian society.
- Under a succession of Tsarist ministers (Bunge, Witte and Stolypin) railways were built, foreign investment attracted and landholdings reformed.
- Economic growth rates averaged 9 per cent from 1894–1900 and 5 per cent from 1900–1914. These were huge rates of change.
- **Industrial growth was centred on armaments** because Tsar Nicholas II wanted to protect Russia's position as a great power. However, oil, textiles, minerals and iron and steel were the industries most affected by economic growth.

By 1914 the Russian economy had grown more slowly than those of Germany, the USA, France and Britain. However, Russia put a huge army of 3 million troops on to the front against Germany and Austria. This meant that Russia was unable to equip her troops as well as her enemies. The strain of supplying them would be immense.

Politics under the Tsar

AQA B
EDEXCEL A
OCR B
WJEC A
NICCEA

 **KEY POINT** **Tsardom: the Tsar was an autocrat. He ruled without any check on his power. He thought he had a special relationship with God.**

Tsar refusing to change

In 1913 the Romanovs celebrated 300 years on the throne. Nicholas II was educated by his father (Alexander III) and his tutor (Pobedonostsev) to believe that no rule other than Tsardom was possible.

No Cabinet government Individual members of the Council of State were sworn to be loyal to the Tsar so the Council could not make decisions of its own. The civil service was well known for time wasting, was open to bribery and treated the people badly.	**Repression** The mounted Cossacks, who used knouts and swords, the Okhrana (secret police) and the army backed up the police. In 1905 the army shot at a demonstration on Bloody Sunday and started a revolution. The Tsar only survived because the army stayed loyal and he made concessions.	**No democracy** The Tsar's 1905 October Manifesto promised a Duma (an assembly). This was never able to force the Tsar to change any policies. Four Dumas were called before 1917. Each had less power and represented a narrower band of society.

Opposition to Tsarist rule

AQA B
EDEXCEL A
OCR B
WJEC A
NICCEA

Though the Dumas were powerless, accounts of their debates could be printed, overturning centuries of political censorship and popularising opposition parties.

Octobrists

The Octobrists were a conservative group who supported the October Manifesto. In 1913 they were led by Guchkov. Although they were the Tsar's most loyal supporters, they thought he had gone too far in removing the Duma's rights, given initially in 1905. They warned that there would be a catastrophe if the Tsar did not make government more respected.

Kadets

The Kadet Party (Constitutional Democrats) was the Liberal group in the Duma. It was led by Milyukov. It represented many middle-class professionals and businessmen, who wanted a constitutional monarchy. This would mean the Tsar and his government would have to answer to a democratic Duma.

Social Democrats

 KEY POINT Communists called themselves Social Democrats at this stage, but were split into several different groups. All believed in Karl Marx's historical interpretation of politics.

In 1903 the Socialists had split into the **Mensheviks** (Men of the Minority) led by Martov, and the **Bolsheviks** (Men of the Majority) led by Lenin. They were supported mainly by the industrial working class. Their leadership was mainly middle class.

The Mensheviks represented the majority of Socialists. They **concentrated on making life better for the working masses**.

> They were not opposed to revolution, but did not think it had to happen before conditions could be improved.

The Bolsheviks were in the minority. Lenin said conditions should not be improved in the present because this would lessen support for revolution. Revolution was the most important aim. Revolution would be followed by a period of change in which society and the economy would be put right (socialism), followed by a communist future.

Socialist Revolutionaries

The Socialist Revolutionaries, led by Chernov, enjoyed **mass support from the peasantry**. **They were the most popular party** in Russia. Some believed in assassinations to weaken the government; many believed in revolution. They were united in their **determination to redistribute land** so everyone would have a fair share.

PROGRESS CHECK

1. In what way did the Tsars try to change the Russian economy from 1855–1914?
2. Why was the Duma not a constitutional government?
3. What was the difference between the Bolsheviks and the Mensheviks?

1. They tried to industrialise it. 2. Because the Tsar did not need to take any notice of it. 3. The Bolsheviks did not seek improvements in society in the present; they wanted to speed up revolution in the future.

11.2 The impact of the First World War

LEARNING SUMMARY

After studying this section you will know:

- *how the First World War was not the short war Russia expected*
- *the ways in which the strain of war showed up the weaknesses in the Russian state*
- *that Nicholas II's efforts to improve Russia's effectiveness in battle were nearly successful*
- *why collapse occurred at home*

The war's effects

AQA B
EDEXCEL A
OCR B
WJEC A
NICCEA

In August 1914 the Russian army mobilised much more quickly than the Germans had expected. Reinforcements had to be switched from the Western Front (the Schlieffen Plan) to the East, weakening the German thrust into France. However, at the battles of Tannenburg and the Masurian Lakes, the Russian army was beaten and forced to give up Poland.

In 1915 the Russian army suffered a severe shell and rifle shortage, partly as a result of the West's failure to supply as promised. Russia made immense efforts to put this right. This probably contributed towards the revolution.

> **But it was weakened further when Romania surrendered later that year.**

By 1916 the Russian army was recovering. Under Brusilov, it fought the only successful offensive of the year.

In early 1917, Russian generals were confident that the shortages were over and expected a successful year. However, the March Revolution destroyed troop morale and the planned offensive against Austro-Hungary was a fiasco.

Russia had been expecting a short war and was not ready for the severe strain of a 'war of attrition'.

- The government was forced to spend more money than it took in taxes. This created **inflation** (money was worth less). **Workers had fixed wages and peasants received fixed prices** for their produce, so they quickly became poorer.

> **He began to solve the supply difficulties, leaving General Alexeev in operational command.**

- **Nicholas II went to the army HQ at Mogilev in 1915** and took over command from his uncle, Grand Duke Nicholas.
- In Petrograd (St Petersburg) **the Tsarina, Alexandra, was left in charge of government**. She was unpopular because of her relationship with **Rasputin**, a holy man thought to have miraculous powers of healing Prince Alexei. **She was also a German and suspected of being a spy**.
- The Tsarina was determined not to compromise on home policy. In addition, chaos and economic dislocation increased as transport broke down through the huge strain of supplying the Front.

- Workers began to strike in protest at the long hours of work needed to supply the army. Food was short because the peasants would not sell it at low government prices. The real cost of living shot up, as food was only available on the black market.

Fig 11.1 Found in the archives of the Okhrana after the March Revolution, this cartoon shows the Tsar and Tsarina under the influence of Rasputin.

11.3 March to November 1917

LEARNING SUMMARY

After studying this section you will know:

- *why Russian society collapsed at home, even though no revolutionary group expected it*
- *why the Provisional Government was unlikely to be successful from the beginning*
- *what mistakes the Provisional Government made*

Russia was more and more successful in supplying the Front but **society collapsed at home**.

- Poverty and hard industrial conditions created **fertile ground for socialist agitators**.
- **The peasants** could not survive low prices for food and high war taxation. They **wanted to take over land owned by the nobility**.
- The **professional and industrial middle classes** were upset by the defeats and shortages at the Front. They **wanted a hand in government to run the war more effectively**. Milyukov combined his Kadets with other moderate parties to form a Progressive Bloc in the Duma. They demanded the right to help, but were refused by the Tsar. He realised this would mean constitutional concessions.
- The aristocracy disliked Alexandra's mismanagement and Nicholas's failures. **Prince Yusupov murdered Rasputin in a December 1916 plot**, but the situation did not improve.

The March Revolution 1917

AQA B
EDEXCEL A
OCR B
WJEC A
NICCEA

A winter of poverty and hunger was followed by several bright spring days. There were rumours of bread rationing in Petrograd. The huge Putilov engineering works there had just shut down. Tens of thousands of workers were jobless.

8 March	• An International Women's Day demonstration was taken over by marchers demanding bread.
	• The Duma had been recently dismissed by the Tsar. It carried on debating in the Tauride Palace, criticising the government.
9 March	• The crowds grew more aggressive.
	• Nearly all the industrial plants in the city closed down.
	• There were violent clashes: some demonstrators and soldiers died but the trouble was contained.
10 March	• Orders came from the Tsar at Mogilev to suppress the demonstrations by force.
	• Control of workers' quarters was lost.
	• Troops fired on demonstrators in Znamenski Square: 40 killed; as many wounded.
	• That evening recruits from the Guard regiments, training to go to the Front, mutinied.
12 March	• By 12 March Petrograd was controlled by the 'peasants in uniform'.
	• By the following night Nicholas, marooned in the royal train at Pskov, had abdicated.

They were living in overcrowded conditions and refused to fire on their own people.

Nicholas expected the throne to pass to his brother Michael who refused it.

The Provisional Government

AQA B
EDEXCEL A
OCR B
WJEC A
NICCEA

Dual power

In Petrograd the revolutionary parties finally realised what was happening. They formed a Soviet (Council). This had the loyalty of the army, navy and industrial workers.

The Provisional Government (a small group of Liberal and Socialist politicians led by Prince George Lvov) declared themselves in control. From the beginning they ruled only because the Soviet allowed them.

Problems of the Provisional Government

The economy was in crisis Inflation, a goods shortage and food famine, the breakdown in transport and huge mounting public debt meant a loan had to be negotiated from the Russia's Western allies. This would only be given if Russia stayed in the war.

The Provisional Government did not represent the people It wanted success in the war. Most of the country wanted peace. Members were Liberals with some Social Revolutionaries. They were unrepresentative of the country but they promised elections.

Dual power with the Petrograd Soviet This could only continue if the Provisional Government kept to its agreement. This weakened its control over the army, police and political control in Petrograd. The city became a mix of conflicting political groups.

The Provisional Government then made the situation worse.

- They proclaimed **free speech, freedom of the press and an amnesty for political prisoners**.

- They **delayed redistribution of land** until after a national election for a Constituent Assembly. They **postponed the election**, hoping to win the war and increase their political standing.

This committed Russia to an offensive war.

- **The Liberals were forced out of the government** when the Milyukov Note was leaked.

- They were replaced by Socialist Revolutionaries led by **Oleg Kerensky**, who became Prime Minister.

- They **could not prevent the return** to Petrograd **of Vladimir Ilych Lenin**. He proclaimed total opposition to them in his April Theses. 'Bread, Peace and Land' was a powerful programme which started to gain support. They could find no evidence that he was a German spy and did not imprison him.

- **An offensive against Germany in June 1917** was a fiasco. It led to a retreat. Communist agitation and army desertions were already common.

This ruined their reputation as upholders of liberty.

- In the 'June Days' they put down Bolshevik anti-war demonstrations in Petrograd with force.

- **They did not provide any leadership after June**. The army began to fall apart. Support for the Bolsheviks grew.

- The Commander in Chief of the army, **General Kornilov, tried to take troops to Petrograd to take control in late August**.

They became the patriotic defenders of the revolution.

- The railway workers resisted his coup. This resulted in the arming of the largely Bolshevik Red Guards.

PROGRESS CHECK

1. Which nobleman killed Rasputin?
2. What was 'Dual Power'?
3. What were the results of the failure of the offensive of June 1917?

1. Prince Yusupov. 2. The sharing of power between the Provisional Government and the Petrograd Soviet. 3. The army began to fall apart; support for the Bolsheviks grew.

11.4 Bolshevik victory: November 1917

LEARNING SUMMARY

After studying this section you will know:

- *why the Bolshevik Party was able to profit from the collapse of the Provisional Government*
- *the contributions of Lenin and Trotsky to Bolshevik success*

Lenin

AQA B
EDEXCEL A
OCR B
WJEC A
NICCEA

Subjecting the army and the population to propaganda to create a second, proletarian revolution.

In early April 1917 Lenin predicted the failure of the Provisional Government.

- He disentangled the Bolsheviks from their associations with the Provisional Government
- He provided them with a programme: 'Bread, Peace and Land'.
- He provided them with a strategy.
- Before Lenin was forced back into hiding and exile in June, support for Bolshevism was already growing among the population at large, in the army and in the navy, stationed at nearby Kronstadt.
- Lenin remained the acknowledged leader of the Bolsheviks, though he was 'on the run' and rarely in Petrograd.
- He finally decided on the necessity of revolution in October, overcoming the opposition from Kamenev and Zinoviev.

> **KEY POINT**
>
> In communist terms, the proletariat is the industrial working class. It does not include the free peasantry or the bourgeoisie (the middle class).

Trotsky

AQA B
EDEXCEL A
OCR B
WJEC A
NICCEA

- Trotsky was famous as a Menshevik before he joined the Bolsheviks in June.
- This made him Lenin's second in command. He displaced Stalin.
- He played an important role as the Chairman of the Petrograd Soviet.
- He chaired the Military Revolutionary Committee, which ran the revolution in November.

The Revolution

Power changed hands without a shot being fired. By October the Bolsheviks had majorities in the Petrograd and Moscow Soviets. All they needed to do was withdraw their support from the Provisional Government to make it fall.

Lenin timed this for the meeting of the National Congress of Soviets on 7 November. Menshevik deputies were encouraged to walk out of the Congress, leaving Lenin free to declare that the revolution was the will of the people.

At the same time the Red Guards, who had taken strategic bridges, railway stations and telephone exchanges beforehand, took the Winter Palace and arrested the Provisional Government.

PROGRESS CHECK

1. What was the slogan popularised by the Bolsheviks to sum up Lenin's policy?
2. From which naval base did much of Lenin's support come in June 1917?
3. As chairman of which Soviet committee did Trotsky run the November Revolution?

1. 'Bread, Peace and Land'. 2. Kronstadt 3. The Military Revolutionary Committee

11.5 Bolshevik rule and its impact 1918–1928

LEARNING SUMMARY

After studying this section you will know:

- *how Lenin and the Bolsheviks secured their hold on the country*
- *why the Red (Bolshevik) forces were in such a strong position*
- *why they compromised with the peasantry and allowed the New Economic Policy*
- *why the New Economic Policy failed in the longer term*

The growth of dictatorship

AQA B
EDEXCEL A
OCR B
WJEC A
NICCEA

> Even after a violent take-over in Moscow the new government had no control over the rest of the country.

Lenin and the Bolsheviks did not gain real power immediately after the revolution. The new government was a coalition between the Bolsheviks and the Left Social Revolutionaries.

Declarations on taking power

Lenin immediately issued two decrees. They gave his supporters much of what they expected from the Revolution.

The Decree on Peace

This **called for a just peace with Germany** without losing power or land, or paying reparations.

Trotsky was unable to stop the war without Germany's agreement. As Commissar for Foreign Affairs he relied on a policy of '**no peace, no war**' for the next few weeks.

Then the Germans began to advance again and the Russian Government had to call for peace negotiations. **This meant surrender.**

The Decree on Land

This nationalised all land but **allowed it to be redistributed to the peasants**.

Lenin had taken over the whole Social Revolutionary land programme in a bid to gain popularity with the majority of the population.

The Cheka

In December 1917 Lenin established the Cheka, under Felix Dzerzhinsky. This was a forerunner of the KGB. It had **rights to investigate, try and execute enemies of the state outside normal courts**.

It was used to terrorise and remove opponents, and marks the beginning of the Bolshevik move towards violence.

The Constituent Assembly

Lenin could not refuse to allow elections to the Constituent Assembly. However, the Socialist Revolutionaries won the election. The Bolsheviks came second, with majorities in Petrograd and Moscow. Unless the Bolsheviks took action, the Constituent Assembly would meet in January 1918 and deprive the Bolsheviks of their claim to represent the people.

Deputies were threatened with violence. Bolshevik deputies jeered and disrupted their speeches. When the Socialist Revolutionary majority refused to adopt the entire Bolshevik programme, Lenin walked out with the rest of the Bolshevik deputies. The assembly hall was shut and guarded. The deputies decided they would be safer at home in the provinces.

> **The dispersal of the Constituent Assembly was a major reason for civil war.**

The Treaty of Brest–Litovsk 3 March 1918

The Soviet Government was forced into agreeing to a peace that gave Germany all her demands:

- the Russian army was demobilised
- Finland, Estonia, Latvia and the Ukraine became independent (the Ukraine under German domination)

This angered many patriotic Russians and increased the anti-Soviet forces gathering throughout Russia. A more serious type of civil war replaced the feeble opposition of former Tsarist generals.

> **White means anti-communist.**

'White' governments backed by the Entente powers, Britain, France and the United States, sprang up. The Left Socialist Revolutionaries left the government. They reverted to old tactics: leading Bolsheviks and the German ambassador were assassinated. The Soviet Government resorted to terror, imprisoning or shooting those it considered opponents.

The Civil War

AQA B
EDEXCEL A
OCR B
WJEC A
NICCEA

During the Civil War the power of the Soviets was reduced and that of the Bolshevik dictatorship increased:

- Soviet congresses became less frequent
- the Soviets lost control of the government, which listened more to the Bolshevik Party
- elections to the Soviets gradually stopped

The war

1918	The Soviet government consolidated its control on the **western centre of the country**.
1919	Red Soviet troops **beat back a three-pronged attack** by Kolchak from the east, Denikin from the south and Yudenich from the north-west. This was the Whites' best chance for victory, but their **Western allies abandoned them**. At the end of the year all three armies were pushed back. Only Ukrainian nationalists, the Volunteer army in the Crimea and the Japanese remained in the Far East.

1920	**Poland**, under General Pilsudski, **attacked the Ukraine**. Soviet cavalry, under Tukhachevsky, pushed them back towards Warsaw, but overreached themselves and had to sign a truce giving Poland a slice of Russian territory. This was finalised in the **Treaty of Riga in 1921**. Wrangel's troops were destroyed and had to evacuate the Crimea. The centre of the war passed to the Far East
1921	The Japanese evacuated the Far East. The Kronstadt and Tambov Revolts were put down with force and the Soviet Government was finally left in control.

Why did the Reds win?

Geography

This was to the Red advantage. They defended a central area with cities (Moscow and Petrograd) and the main armaments industries against disunited White forces attacking from the Black Sea, across Siberia and from Latvia.

The railway system was centred on Moscow. This allowed the Reds to switch troops from front to front; the Whites could not. Immense distances had to be crossed to attack this area from the south and east. This signalled any threat early enough for the Reds to pick off their enemies one by one.

Leadership

Trotsky established the Red Army, with Tsarist officers blackmailed into serving faithfully.

Lenin ran the policy of War Communism: the Soviets took the resources they needed at the risk of alienating the peasantry.

Trotsky's charismatic generalship (helped by his armoured train) meant that risky decisions were taken.

For example, in 1919 the Red Army concentrated on destroying Kolchak in Siberia, ignoring Denikin's advance from the south until he was perilously close to Moscow.

White command was not united. White forces frequently fought each other or stood by while the Reds destroyed them piecemeal, as in 1920, when Wrangel and Petliura failed to unite with the Poles.

Propaganda

This favoured the Reds. They used **agitprop** trains to show films, distribute posters and news sheets.

The Reds had the great advantage of having given land to the peasants. The Whites wanted to give it back to the landowners.

In 1918 the Soviet capital moved from Petrograd to Moscow. In 1920 the Bolshevik Party changed its name to the Communist Party.

The Reds were not anti-semitic. The Whites attacked Jewish settlements.

The result was that most peasant guerrilla risings favoured the Reds and destabilised the rear of the White armies. The Reds were seen as a patriotic force, freeing Russia from foreign invaders.

The New Economic Policy (NEP)

AQA B
EDEXCEL A
OCR B
WJEC A
NICCEA

10th Party Congress

> **Communist Government crisis in 1921**
>
> **Economic** By 1921 the peasants were refusing to plant more than they could eat for fear of confiscation. Towns were shrinking: Petrograd had only one–third of its former population. A famine would kill about 5 million Russians by 1922.
>
> **Peasantry** The peasants were alienated by the confiscations of War Communism, and had no real links with the Communist Party. Lenin viewed them as a separate group within the country, with whom his proletariat would have to make an agreement.
>
> **Political** The Communist Party seemed to be splitting up internally between:
> - those who wanted increased Party democracy, but inside the Party structure (Democratic Centralists) and others
> - those who wanted a swift transition to a planned economy and workers' armies (Trotsky, Preobrazhensky)
> - those who wanted more democracy based on Trade Union power (Alexandra Kollontai and the Workers' Opposition)
>
> These 'platforms' threatened the existence of the Party. Its membership was falling and it was isolated within the country.

This was held in Petrograd in March 1921 against a background of crisis. The delegates were used to raise the morale of the troops putting down the Kronstadt Revolt. The peasant uprising in **Tambov** took place at the same time.

The Congress passed two major resolutions.

- **The Syndicalist and Anarchist Deviation** within our Party: this directly criticised the Workers' Opposition.
- **On Party Unity:** defined factions within the Party as 'groups with special platforms ' and called for their immediate dissolution on pain of expulsion. **Party discipline was greatly reinforced**.

> The Congress was blamed for the move towards dictatorship inside the Party after Lenin's death.

The New Economic Policy (NEP)

Lenin enforced a truce with the peasantry. **This was the opposite of War Communism.**

- **Forced requisitioning of farm produce was replaced by a smaller 'tax in kind'** (i.e. tax paid in produce). This allowed peasants to sell their surplus on the free market.
- **Small-scale businesses were denationalised**. This allowed a large sector of the market to return to normal.
- 'The commanding heights of industry' (coal, steel, transport etc.) remained in government hands.
- A purge of Party membership, a reduction in persecution of 'class enemies' and the creation of law codes to allow a return to normal life

Why would the Communist Party dislike the measures of NEP?

Many people in the Communist Party hated these measures. They thought they were compromises. Lenin justified them as **'one step backward in order to take two steps forward'**.

During the NEP, **communist organisation was greatly strengthened**. This made the later move to real dictatorship and centralised control possible.

The Communist Party remained in control and the economy began to recover, but **the NEP was never regarded as a permanent feature**.

The success of the NEP

The NEP seemed a success. It returned the economy to pre-1914 levels and gave the Communist Party the breathing space it needed to survive.

	Index of industrial production	Index of agricultural production
1913	100	100
1921	31	60
1924	45	90
1926	98	118
1928	132	124

The failure of the NEP

They thought the economic disease of capitalism would infect the proletariat.

For the Locarno Pact see Chapter 4 on the League of Nations.

- **Growth slackened after 1926**. Once spare capacity in the economy had been taken up, the NEP did not maximise industrial development. There could be no communist future without industrialisation.

- The **Communist Party could not rely on free enterprise for very long.** They thought it was morally wrong.

- The **Soviet Government was worried about external security.** The Treaty of Locarno 1925 weakened the friendship that had existed between Russia and Germany since Brest–Litovsk. The Soviet Union was worried that capitalist powers would re-invade Russia, especially after Britain broke off relations in May 1927, and communism suffered reverses in China in 1927. There were inescapable connections between defence and industrialisation.

- There were **problems within the economy**, especially the **'scissors crisis'**. From 1923 until 1926 particularly, agricultural output increased faster than industrial output. A 'goods famine' meant the peasantry made large amounts of money but could not spend it. It was difficult to move this money into the development of heavy industry, as the government wished.

PROGRESS CHECK

1. What excuse did Lenin give when he walked out of the Constituent Assembly?
2. Which White general attacked from the south in 1919?
3. Who led the Workers' Opposition in 1921?

1. The Assembly refused to pass the entire Bolshevik programme. 2. General Denikin 3. Alexandra Kollontai

11.6 Stalin's dictatorship

After studying this section you will know:

● *how Stalin was able to take complete control*
● *how far the Soviet Union benefited from industrialisation and collectivisation*
● *how Stalin increased his hold on the Communist Party through the purges*

The leadership struggle

AQA B
EDEXCEL A
OCR B
NICCEA

In 1918 Lenin was shot twice by a Socialist Revolutionary, Dora Kaplan. He seemed to recover but suffered a stroke in May 1922.

He returned to work in October, suffered a second stroke in December, a third in March 1923 and a final stroke in January 1924. From 1923 to his death in 1924, Lenin was seriously disabled.

During this time Lenin's well-being was in the hands of Josef Stalin. He was deputed by the Politburo to provide for his recovery.

Stalin and the General Secretaryship

Stalin made a serious political mistake when, as Commissar for Nationalities, he used force to subdue the Georgian Communist Party in 1921. A new post was found for him in April 1922 as General Secretary of the Communist Party. This was not a promotion. It was a step down to an administrative post.

The strain of the General Secretaryship had killed Yakov Sverdlov, the first Secretary.

However, the General Secretaryship was crucial in the power struggles following Lenin's retirement:

> Within the Communist Party's structure, the Central Committee was supposed to be most powerful organisation. In fact, its important decisions were made in its committees: the Politburo for policy, the Orgburo for party organisation and personnel, and the Secretariat for business organisation.

● it brought membership of the three crucial organisations that ruled the Party: the Politburo, Orgburo and Secretariat
● in charge of the Orgburo, Stalin directed personnel to carry out Politburo decisions and filled positions within the Party hierarchy
● as Secretary, Stalin controlled the flow of information to the Politburo, wrote its agendas and minutes and controlled many other areas of Party organisation

Fig 11.2 Lenin and Stalin in 1922, during Lenin's first illness. This picture was used by Stalin to demonstrate their 'closeness'. Its truthfulness has been questioned.

The struggle against Trotsky

Trotsky was the most able member of the leadership but he was disliked because:

- he had only joined the Bolshevik Party in June 1917, when success was already likely
- he had not served a long apprenticeship as others had within the Party
- he was arrogant and insensitive
- many thought that he would take over when Lenin died and become a dictator

Ranged against Trotsky in the Politburo in 1923 was the **Troika** of Stalin, Zinoviev and Kamenev.

> Trotsky was seen as a Napoleonic figure because he was Commissar for War and had heroic standing in the Party.

Bureaucratisation

In a letter to the Central Committee in late 1923, Trotsky criticised the lack of democracy within the Party, the practice of filling key posts through nomination by the Orgburo and the dominance of full-time officials.

This attack on the Party bureaucracy was supported by the so-called 'Platform of the 46', a group of dissatisfied Congress members. It directly criticised the power of the Troika.

'Socialism in One Country'

Lenin and Trotsky had always maintained that the victory of socialism in Russia would be accompanied by world revolution. By 1923, however, it looked increasingly unlikely that communist revolution would sweep Europe.

Stalin argued that socialism could be achieved in Russia independently of international revolution. By showing his belief in the Russian proletariat, he won most of the Communist Party over to his side.

On 17 January 1925 Trotsky was removed as War Commissar. He kept his membership of the Politburo.

The struggle against the Left opposition

In 1925 the Troika fell apart. Zinoviev and Kamenev recognised that Stalin, not Trotsky, was the greatest threat to their own leadership ambitions.

In 1925 Zinoviev published *Leninism: An Introduction to the Study of Leninism.* He no longer supported the NEP and now attacked 'Socialism in One Country', supporting Trotsky's view of the importance of international revolution.

Stalin packed the 14th Congress, held in December 1925, with his own supporters. He defeated Kamenev and Zinoviev's group.

The struggle against the united opposition

> These former enemies could never agree on positive policies and their presence on one platform only showed their own ambition.

At the 14th Congress Zinoviev had called for all oppositionists who had left active Party life to combine to oppose Stalin.

An alliance between Trotsky, Zinoviev and Kamenev was tried. It was unsuccessful.

Trotsky and Kamenev were removed from their Politburo membership in October 1926 after denunciation from the Party and press.

In early 1927 they organised public demonstrations against the government. Stalin had Kamenev and Trotsky expelled from the Party in December 1927.

Trotsky was sent into internal exile at Alma Ata and, a year later, into foreign exile. Kamenev and Zinoviev were sent to Kaluga but readmitted to the Party the next year.

The struggle against the Right opposition

In January and February 1928 Stalin resorted to forcible grain collection. He was criticised in private by Bukharin, Rykov and Tomsky, who also condemned his policy of rapid industrialisation.

The conflict continued in private in 1928 and 1929. The Right was steadily undermined.

Stalin was left supreme. All the leaders with potential support in the lower ranks of the Party had been routed.

By late 1929 Stalin and his supporters launched a campaign of denunciation in the press. The opposition signed a reversal of their views. The Central Committee removed Bukharin from the Politburo and censured Rykov and Tomsky.

Collectivisation

AQA B
EDEXCEL A
OCR B
NICCEA

By 1928 the peasants were refusing to supply grain in the quantities necessary to feed the towns because they could not buy goods in exchange.

Stalin sent out requisitioning squads in a return to the practices of War Communism. This made the problem worse and effectively ending the NEP. He did this because:

- he saw the peasantry as an opposition group; they had never joined the Communist Party in large numbers
- he blamed profiteering by peasants for their refusal to supply grain, specifically the **Kulaks** (prosperous peasants)
- he needed to confiscate capital to pay for industrial change and the beginning of the Five-Year Plan

He wanted to:

- destroy private agriculture, forcibly establish collective farms and reduce peasants to tied agricultural workers
- destroy the Kulaks as a class

By taking over all agriculture he thought he would be able to run it more efficiently, supply grain to the towns more steadily and export grain in exchange for agricultural machinery. The government would dominate the countryside as never before.

This policy was unplanned, ill-informed and carried out in a confused way. In January 1930 the Central Committee said collectivisation had to be completed in major grain-producing areas by autumn 1930 or spring 1931. In other areas the deadline was autumn 1931 or spring 1932 at the latest.

Results of collectivisation

AQA B
EDEXCEL A
OCR B
NICCEA

- There was a myth of popular enthusiasm for the policy. In fact, it met resentment and even armed opposition.
- Collectivisation was carried out forcibly: village buildings were destroyed and Kulaks arrested.
- The chaos was so great that, in March 1930, Stalin had to call a temporary halt. This meant that the proportion of the peasantry in the new collective farms fell by 60 per cent in three months. The process was restarted after the harvest.
- Peasants destroyed livestock, produce and tools rather than surrender them to the state.
- Extensive grain procurements and a reduction in production led to famine in the Ukraine and North Caucasus in 1933. As many as 10 million people may have died.
- Party control over the countryside was established and private ownership destroyed. Internal passports were reintroduced in 1932.
- Land was nationalised and production targets and delivery quotas set by the state. Never again would the peasantry hold the state to ransom.
- From 1935 private plots of land were allowed. By 1937 these produced 50 per cent to 70 per cent of marketable vegetables, fruit, meat and milk.

	Index	Grain harvest	Cattle	Pigs	Sheep	Goats
1913	100					
1928	124	74.5 m tonnes	60.1 m	22.0 m	97.3 m	9.7 m
1933	101	69.5	33.5	9.9	34.0	3.3
1936	109	57.0	46.0	25.9	43.8	6.1
1940	141	97.1	47.8	22.5	66.6	11.1

Industrialisation

AQA B
EDEXCEL A
OCR B
NICCEA

The Five-Year Plans were intended to:

- provide **machinery** (e.g. tractors), to mechanise farming
- **catch up with the Western world** so Russia would be less dependent on the West for industrial goods
- ensure a strong armaments industry so Russia could defend herself

Stalin believed in state planning. The state would decide what was to be produced and how, when and where. It would decide prices and wages. Stalin decided on three Five-Year Plans.

First Five-Year Plan 1928–1932

- This emphasised heavy industry (coal, oil, iron and steel, electricity) to lay the foundations for future industrial advance.
- A total of 1,500 new industrial plants and 100 new towns were built.

Fig. 11.3 A Soviet poster of 1929: enemies of the Five-Year Plan.

Second Five-Year Plan 1933–1937

- Heavy industry remained top priority, but communications, especially railways, were important.
- Chemicals and metallurgy industries grew enormously.

Third Five-Year Plan 1938–1941 (cut short by the war)

- More and more resources switched into armaments: tanks, planes and weapons.

Effects of the Five-Year Plans

	Total index	Producer goods index	Consumer goods index
1913	100	100	100
1928	132	155	120
1932	267	424	187
1933	281	450	196
1937	588	1013	373
1938	657	1138	415
1940	852	1554	497

There was:

- a huge increase in the production of industry

- a huge increase in the number of railways, canals (Belomore Canal), dams (Dneipr Dam), gigantic factories (Stalingrad Tractor Works) and new cities (Magnetogorsk) built

- a variety of social changes:
  - the urban population more than doubled
  - more than nine million peasants left the land during the First Five-Year Plan alone: squalid urban conditions, poor transport and services and a serious housing shortage resulted

- lack of jobs reduced workers' discipline, but the sabotage scare introduced fear into the workplace. The Stakhanovite movement 1935–1936 tried to stimulate workers by producing positive role models

Within the economy, industry became the dominant sector and the government the dominant power.

Stalin's purges

AQA B
EDEXCEL A
OCR B
NICCEA

Stalin consolidated his power as dictator of the Soviet Union in much the same way as Hitler did in Germany. He exerted totalitarian control through:

- terror imposed through secret police and labour camps
- state control of education, arts and sciences, propaganda and censorship
- a single-party state

During the 1930s the huge disruption to the population and economic life caused by industrialisation and collectivisation created great political controversy, but Stalin secured his position by making it too dangerous to criticise the government publicly. He extended his terror into the factories (in his campaigns against sabotage) and against party rivals (in the Great Purges).

Sergei Kirov

Petrograd was renamed Leningrad in 1924.

Kirov had been popular in Leningrad since the 1920s.

In 1934, when the collectivisation crisis was over, many thought it was time to slow down economic change and improve relations with the peasantry. Kirov championed these views at the 17th Party Congress and emerged as the popular alternative to Stalin. Shortly afterwards he was shot inside the Party offices in Leningrad.

Stalin gave him a state funeral, but there is no doubt who was responsible. The murder was the excuse for a spate of arrests.

The 1936 purges

In the show trials, watched by the world, they confessed to laughable charges, such as that they had tried to murder Lenin.

In 1936 Stalin began a greater purge of all those he suspected within the Party.

Zinoviev and Kamenev were accused with 14 others of the murder of Kirov and of supporting Trotsky.

Despite their 'confessions', Zinoviev, Kamenev and the others were executed.

Later purges

Thousands of other Communist Party members were denounced from 1936–1938.

In 1937 there were show trials of senior officials accused of sabotage and spying. In 1938 Bukharin, Rykov and Yagoda were shot.

Results of the purges

- Over one-fifth of the membership of the Communist Party were expelled or shot.
- Of 1,961 delegates to the 17th Party Congress in 1934, 1,108 were arrested.
- Of 139 Central Committee members, over 90 were shot.
- Five out of 11 Politburo members were shot in 1934.
- Marshall Tukhachevsky and seven other generals, heroes of the Civil War, were shot.
- 90 per cent of all Soviet generals and thousands of army and airforce officers were shot or imprisoned: this left Soviet armed forces in a desperate situation at the beginning of the Second World War.
- The purges ended in 1938 but by 1939 it is estimated that over 20 million Russians had been transported to labour camps.
- Stalin's position was unchallengeable.

PROGRESS CHECK

1. By what name was the opposition to Trotsky in 1923 known?
2. Which peasant group did Stalin destroy as a class?
3. Name three great constructions of the Five-Year Plans.

1. The Troika 2. The Kulaks 3. Belomore Canal, Dnepir Dam, Stalingrad Tractor Works, Magnetogorsk.

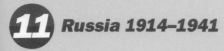

Exam practice questions

1.

(a) What was collectivisation? **(4)**

....

....

....

....

....

....

(b) Explain why Stalin introduced the Five-Year Plans. **(6)**

....

....

....

....

....

....

....

(c) Stalin made changes in industry and agriculture. Which were the most important – the industrial or the agricultural changes? Explain your answer. **(10)**

....

....

....

....

....

....

....

....

....

OCR Specimen Paper

12 Germany 1918–1945

The following topics are covered in this chapter:

- The weakness of the Weimar Republic
- Hitler's rise to power
- Nazi control of Germany 1933-1945
- Life in Nazi Germany

12.1 The weakness of the Weimar Republic

LEARNING SUMMARY

After studying this section you will know:

- how defeat gave the new German Republic little chance of success
- how the Weimar Republic was able to survive during its first disastrous years
- how Gustav Stresemann helped to restore stability in the mid-1920s
- how weak the Republic remained when it was struck by the Wall Street Crash in 1929

Defeat caused a Socialist Weimar Republic

AQA B
OCR B
NICCEA

Defeat

Germany had refused President Wilson's Fourteen Points and in 1918 gambled on her first major offensive since 1914, the Ludendorff Offensive. The result was disastrous. By November she could fight no more and was forced to accept the terms of the Armistice on 11 November.

Disaster

The end of The First World War and the Treaty of Versailles are explained in detail on pages 40–43.

The Kaiser had fled to Holland. Ludendorff organised a parliamentary republic, but also thought Germany had been let down by the Socialists and war profiteers, who would now form the new government.

Background to surrender

This is the origin of Hitler's myth of the 'stab in the back'.

- Germany had **lost 2 million men** during the war, with over **6 million wounded**.
- Her **currency had lost 75 per cent of its value** between 1913 and 1918.
- Germany was **split between the extremes** of the Independent Socialist Party on the left and the Fatherland Party on the right.

- After the 'turnip winter' of 1917–1918, Germany suffered a major flu epidemic, Thousands died at its height. **In 1918 293,000 people died from starvation and hypothermia.**

Revolution

- October 1918: the **sailors of Kiel and Wilhelmshaven mutinied**. Prince Max of Baden handed power to Freidrich Ebert, a moderate Socialist, to try to maintain control while agreeing to the surrender.
- January 1919: a further wave of **Spartacist (communist) unrest** made it impossible to convene the new National Assembly in Berlin. It met at Weimar, in February 1919, and had drawn up the Weimar Constitution by August.

> **KEY POINT** The Weimar Republic refers to government under the Weimar Constitution. It does not refer to a political party.

The impact of the Treaty of Versailles on the Republic

AQA B
OCR B
NICCEA

The new Weimar Republic had to shoulder the blame for the disastrous Treaty of Versailles.

The Treaty of Versailles

> Adolf Hitler called The Treaty of Versailles a diktat.

Germany rejected it but was forced to sign it in June 1919.

- **Millions of Germans were given to neighbouring states** and **Germany was left with too few soldiers to defend herself.**
- The German Government had been excluded from the negotiations and the treaty imposed. It was a '**diktat**' (a dictated peace).

> The final reparations bill was decided in 1921: a staggering £6,600 million in gold or manufactured goods.

- **War guilt** was imposed on Germany to justify making her pay **reparations** to the Allies.

Political instability

The Weimar Republic was blamed for Germany's humiliation at Versailles, which weakened the new democracy. Its first years were troubled by constant instability.

January and March 1919	**Spartacist rising** in Berlin: more than 1,200 killed by the army under General Groener. A Soviet Republic was declared in Bavaria.
March 1920	**Wolfgang Kapp** led rightist nationalist Freikorps (disbanded soldiers) in their bid for power in Berlin. They were defeated by a general strike. The communists formed the Ruhr Army (50,000 workers) to resist the Freikorps and the army. Ebert granted concessions, then used the army. Over 1,000 workers and 250 police were killed by 1923.
June 1922	Assassination of the Foreign Minister, Walther Rathenau, by right-wing terrorists. They disliked his Jewish origins and he had attempted to improve the Treaty of Versailles.
January 1923	French and Belgian troops invaded the Ruhr to extract reparations by force.
Summer 1923	Economic collapse followed by communist strikes in Saxony. Suppressed by government troops in October.
November 1923	The Munich Putsch (see page 148).

Constitutional problems

The Weimar Republic was also undermined by its own constitution. It was based on proportional representation and could not provide support for strong measures. Socialist support fell from 38 per cent in 1919 to 21 per cent in 1920.

> **KEY POINT**
>
> Proportional representation and coalition government: members of the Reichstag were elected in exactly the same proportion as the votes cast for them in the election. This often led to weak coalition governments.

Hyper-inflation

> **KEY POINT**
>
> Hyper-inflation is rapidly accelerating inflation in which prices rise ten or a hundred-fold within a month.

In 1923 the German mark lost its value. War debts, the impossibility of selling goods to a poverty stricken population and the invasion of the Ruhr by the French and the Belgians had destroyed the economy.

		Marks to the $
1914		4.2
1919		8.9
1920		14.0
1922		191.8
1923	Jan	17,792
	Jul	353,412
	Sep	98,860,000
	Nov	200,000,000,000

The recovery of the Weimar Republic 1923–1929

AQA B
OCR B
NICCEA

During this period the Republic seemed to overcome its difficulties.

Gustav Stresemann 1878–1929

In August 1923 Gustav Stresemann, the leader of the German People's Party, became Chancellor. He:

- put down communist governments in Saxony and Thuringia
- ended the hyper-inflationary crisis by issuing the **Rentenmark** (in November 1923)
- defeated Hitler's Munich Putsch

Although his government fell, Stresemann remained influential as Foreign Minister:

- April 1924 – re-organised reparations in Germany's favour in the **Dawes Plan** (see page 146)
- 1925 – made peace with France in the **Locarno Treaty** guaranteeing that each country was safe from invasion by the other and finally sending home French troops from the Ruhr.

Details of the Locarno Treaty can be found on page 52.

- 1926 – took Germany into the **League of Nations**
- June 1929 – renegotiated the foreign loans in the **Young Plan**

Prosperity began to look secure. Then in October 1929 Stresemann died. On 29 October came the Wall Street Crash, which plunged Germany and the world into the Depression.

The Dawes Plan 1924–29

This was negotiated by the Allies and bankers organised by the American Charles Dawes.

The plan:

- did not reduce the huge reparations bill set in 1921
- reduced the initial payments to allow German industry to re-equip itself
- allowed reparations schedules to be met by loans
- helped stabilise the new Rentenmark
- said that after five years a second negotiation would decide on repayment of loans and reparations

The plan bump-started the German economy, at the expense of the country raising even larger loans. During this period more was lent to Germany than was repaid. Germany seemed better off in the short term.

The Young Plan 1929–1932

- reduced the reparations from 132,000 to 37,000 million marks
- annual payments, lower than in the Dawes Plan, spread over 58 years
- Allied control of the railways, Reichsbank and customs duties stopped
- Allied troops finally withdrawn from Germany

The weaknesses of the Weimar period

The Weimar period lasted until Hitler became Chancellor in January 1933, but the last years (1929–1933) were a time of increasing economic and political crisis (see pages 150–151).

- **The early years of democracy had shown that the Weimar Republic was weak** and could be coerced. Hindenburg, who became President in 1926 when Ebert died, was one of many who did not believe in democracy.

- **The Dawes Plan stabilised the regime but at the cost of mortgaging the future** and persuading many that the Allies should not be bought off by agreeing to the Versailles Settlement.

- **Prosperity was uneven.** There was an unemployment crisis in 1926; the rate of industrial growth was low; and the country was unable to pay in the long term for an ambitious welfare state.

---

1. Give three reasons why the Weimar Republic was weak in 1919.
2. What three disasters struck the Republic in 1923?
3. What weaknesses remained by 1928?

PROGRESS CHECK

1. The army was too small to keep order; the Socialist Government was too weak to impose policies; and the government was blamed for the Treaty of Versailles. 2. The Belgian and French invasion of the Ruhr; hyper-inflation; and the Munich Putsch. 3. Many people did not believe in democracy; economic progress was uneven; the Dawes Plan had mortgaged the country's future; the government had promised too much.

12.2 Hitler's rise to power

LEARNING SUMMARY

After studying this section you will know:

● how Hitler's early life prepared him to become leader of Germany
● why the Nazi Party gained little success in the 1920s but much during the Depression
● what led to Hitler becoming Chancellor of Germany
● how Hitler was able to move from being Chancellor to Führer between 1933 and 1934

His early life

AQA B
EDEXCEL A
OCR B
WJEC A   WJEC B
NICCEA

Munich is in Bavaria, a state in southern Germany.

● Adolf Hitler was an Austrian Catholic born in 1889.
● At first he worked hard, but later became unmanageable and left school early, in 1905.
● He drifted to Vienna, where he failed to gain a place at the Vienna Academy of Fine Arts, and then to Munich in 1913.
● When war was declared in 1914 he quickly joined a Bavarian regiment.

His army career

In the German army, Hitler found his purpose in life.

● He was an exemplary soldier, a battalion messenger.
● He won the Iron Cross twice.
● He rose only to corporal because he was thought to lack leadership qualities.
● He was wounded in 1916, gassed in 1918 and in hospital when he heard of Germany's defeat.

How he joined the Nazi Party

● He was an 'education officer' in the Bavarian army's political section.
● He joined **Anton Drexler's** German Workers' Party (DAP).
● In February 1920 Hitler and Drexler drew up the Twenty-five Point Programme and changed the party's name to the Nazi Party.

What the Nazi Party stood for in the 1920s

AQA B
EDEXCEL A
OCR B
WJEC A   WJEC B
NICCEA

> **KEY POINT**   Anti-semitism means hatred of Jews.

The Nazi Party Twenty-five Point Programme

This showed the Nazi Party believed in:

- anti-semitism
- survival of the fittest race
- German nationalism
- authoritarian leadership

The Munich Beer Hall Putsch

> **KEY POINT**   Putsch means the taking of power by a small, armed group – a coup d'état.

By 1923 the Nazi Party had 55,000 members in Bavaria. It had its own paramilitary force, the SA. Hitler was disgusted that Stresemann negotiated payment of reparations, apparently agreeing to the Versailles Treaty. He tried to take power in Bavaria.

8 November	Hitler and his SA burst into a meeting held by General von Lossow (Army commander in Bavaria) and Gustav von Kahr (Head of State of Bavaria) in a beer hall in Munich.
	• He demanded their support for his seizure of power and his replacement of von Lossow with General Ludendorff as army commander.
	• Thousands of SA arrested other members of the Bavarian Government, but failed to gain control of the army barracks.
9 November	• President Ebert declared a national state of emergency.
	• Ludendorff persuaded Hitler to march into Munich as the first step to Berlin.
	• A total of 2,000 SA marched towards the military base in Munich. Armed police and soldiers met them: 14 Nazis were killed.
	• Hitler fled: Ludendorff was arrested.
11 November	• Hitler arrested; Nazis banned.

To find out why Ludendorff was famous, see Chapter 2 on the First World War.

Mein Kampf, My Struggle, was published in 1925. It was a mixture of autobiography and statement of beliefs and aims. From 1933 it was Germany's best-selling book. Hitler grew wealthy on the profits.

Hitler on trial

In early 1924 Hitler was tried for treason. He turned the trial into a platform from which to attack the Weimar Government.

The trial, just before the elections, allowed the Nazis to become the third largest group in Bavaria.

Ludendorff was acquitted, Hitler was sentenced to the minimum five years in prison. He was released in December 1924 after only nine months. He had used the time to write *Mein Kampf.*

Nazi failure before 1930

AQA B
EDEXCEL A
OCR B
WJEC A   WJEC B
NICCEA

The Nazi Party made little headway during the 1920s when the Weimar Republic was strong.

Strength of the moderate parties in the Weimar Republic

- After 1923 the Weimar Republic was more stable, with no attempted coups or assassinations between 1924 and 1929.
- After 1924, voters switched back to voting for the moderate parties, which supported the Weimar Constitution.
- The government was strengthened when the Nationalist Party (DNVP) representing the most influential and propertied part of the population and the army, had thrown its weight behind the Constitution.
- Hindenburg, the new President, did not really believe in the Republic, but was under oath to protect it.

Change of tactics

After his release from prison Hitler changed Nazi Party tactics away from revolution and towards gaining democratic control. He:

- took supreme power over the party – asserted the **Leadership Principle**, re-organised the party's structure, strategy and symbols (e.g. he designed the **swastika flag)**
- used Weimar democracy to gain control rather than another putsch

Local grievances were addressed by local speakers.

- used propaganda to target specific grievances
- used the Nazi Party's newspaper, the **Völkischer Beobachter,** to spread its ideas
- extended party organisation throughout Germany, and so changed the emphasis of the Party from being a southern German and specifically Bavarian party, to being a national party

The Nazi Party had concentrated its efforts in Bavaria, in southern Germany, which was largely Catholic. The Catholic Church had its own party, the Centre. When the Nazis extended their efforts into Protestant, agricultural and small town areas in the north of Germany (Schleswig-Holstein) they began to have success.

- developed a powerful message. He:
  - stressed the national community of all Germans
  - promised to solve economic problems and provide bread
  - paid special attention to small traders and peasants, who would be saved from 'the clutch of the Jewish moneylenders'
  - promised to smash the Weimar Constitution and provide strong leadership
  - preached nationalism and promised to destroy the Versailles Treaty

These strategies eventually brought success, but not until the Weimar Republic was destroyed by the Depression.

Success in elections 1928–1933

> This was because it was so dependent on foreign loans and because the government was indecisive.

Changes in Nazi tactics and the growth of unemployment transformed Nazi fortunes.

The effects of the Wall Street Crash on Germany

By 1929 Hitler and the Nazi Party were well placed to benefit from any disaster the ruling coalition suffered. Between 1929 and 1932 the Depression hit Germany particularly hard.

	1929	1932
Unemployment (millions)	1.4	5.6
Wages (1913 = 100)	169	113
Government income 1928-1929 (bn RM)	9.0	6.6
Government expenditure on welfare services (per person in marks)	102	106

> Between the elections of May 1928 and July 1932, the percentage of votes cast for the Nazi Party in Reichstag elections leapt from 2.6 to 37.4 per cent.

No one could afford to buy goods. Unemployment rose but unemployment pay was cut. This caused major disagreements and the fall of the government.

Although government expenditure on welfare services increased little, its income fell by one-third. By 1933 Germany appeared bankrupt.

 KEY POINT — Deflation is the opposite of inflation. Goods become worth less because there are too many of them.

The weakness of the government

Between March 1930 and January 1933, **none of the three governments of Brüning, Papen and Schleicher was able to rule with a majority** in the Reichstag. President Hindenburg had to use his powers under the Weimar Constitution to rule by decree. This was because parties did not agree about whether to tax workers or employers to pay the unemployed. Others argued that unemployment benefits should be cut.

In 1930 Chancellor **Brüning called an election**. There were remarkable gains for the Nazi and Communist Parties, and this **made the Reichstag even more unmanageable**.

Although **President Hindenburg** acted constitutionally, it is quite clear **he preferred to rule by decree** than allow the Communist or Nazi parties into power. He refused Hitler's demand to be made Chancellor.

Hitler's tactics

● He **gained support from industrialists** such as Alfred Hugenburg and Fritz Thyssen because of their reaction against the Young Plan. This provided money and media coverage. However, most financial support still came from ordinary people's contributions at meetings.

By 1930 the SA was a huge army of young men, with ex-soldiers. Led by Ernst Röhm, they were provided with free brown shirts, meals and sometimes accommodation in hostels. They distributed propaganda leaflets, protected Nazi meetings from disruption and tried to destroy the communists.

- The **Sturm-Abteilung (SA), founded in 1920, gave invaluable support**. They provided over 100 'martyrs' to the cause and focused attention against the Communists. Their disciplined militarism attracted the German people.

- **Hitler, himself, was important to Nazi success**. He refused to co-operate with any other party unless he was given the Chancellorship and power to rule without the Reichstag. Support for the Nazis rose in each election.

- He used the latest technology: loudspeakers, slide shows, films and the first aerial political campaign 'Führer over Germany' in the 1932 presidential election.

- He used his own oratorical power to sway vast crowds.

The bargain that brought Hitler to power

April 1932

- President **Hindenburg** was re-elected president. He **dismissed Brüning's government**. The new government, under **Papen**, **had support from less than 10 per cent of the electorate**. In an election in July the Communist and Nazis Parties won over half the Reichstag seats between them.

- **Hitler demanded to be made Chancellor**. He also demanded an Enabling Act to allow him to rule by decree (reducing the President's power). Hindenburg refused.

- **Papen could not control the new Reichstag, which was suspended after one day.**

Papen wanted to rule without the Reichstag, but Schleicher, leader of the Nationalists, tried to create a 'diagonal front' uniting some parts of the trades unions and the Nazis. Schleicher persuaded Hindenburg to dismiss Papen and appoint himself Chancellor, but his attempts to unite right and left failed. Hindenburg rejected Schleicher's request to be allowed to rule by decree.

November 1932

- There was another election. **The Nazi vote fell to 33 per cent.**

- The new Reichstag was as impossible to control as the old.

- Papen constructed a government around Hitler. **Hitler would be Chancellor**, Papen Vice Chancellor, and General von Blomberg Defence Minister (for army support).

- Hindenburg had no alternative but to appoint Hitler Chancellor, but neither he nor Papen appreciated that they would become puppets.

KEY POINT   Hitler came to power through a plot. Democracy was not working even before he destroyed it.

Hitler's consolidation of power 1933–1934

AQA B
EDEXCEL A
OCR B
WJEC A   WJEC B
NICCEA

30 January 1933	Hitler appointed Chancellor	Only three Nazis in the government
27 February	Reichstag fire	Probably started by Dutch communist van der Lubbe acting alone, but Hitler blamed it on the Communist Party
28 February	Decree of the Reich President for the protection of the nation and the state	● Hindenburg suspended all civil rights ● people could be held indefinitely in protective custody ● used to repress the Communist Party
5 March	Elections	● Nazi opponents intimidated ● Nazis won 44 per cent of the vote. Their allies, the Nationalists, gained 8 per cent
24 March	Enabling Act	● The Reichstag met in the Opera House. Members were intimidated by SA and SS ● Gave emergency powers to the government to issue decrees and rule without the Reichstag for four years
7 April	Law for the restoration of the professional civil service	The first anti-Jewish measure: Jews and other 'aliens' purged from administration, courts, schools and universities
1 May	May Day holiday	International Labour Day made a public holiday. The day after, trades union offices were abolished
14 July	Law against the formation of new parties	Germany became a one-party state
12 November	New elections	Nazi Party won 92 per cent of the vote
January 1934	Law for the reconstruction of the state	State governments overthrown and replaced by Nazi governors
30 June	Night of the Long Knives	SS shot many SA leaders and others (e.g. Schleicher) seen as a threat
2 August	Death of President Hindenburg	Hitler became Führer (Chancellor and President: Leader)

THEY SALUTE WITH BOTH HANDS NOW

PROGRESS CHECK

1. What were the four main policies in the Nazi Party programme of 1921?
2. List five important changes in Nazi tactics in the late 1920s.
3. Name the three main characters in the cartoon. What event does it show?

1. Anti-semitism; survival of the fittest (Social Darwinism); German nationalism; authoritarian leadership 2. To gain control through democracy; the Leadership Principle; local issues; national campaigning; powerful message 3. Hitler, Goebbels, Goering; The Night of the Long Knives – Hitler had just taken power over the SA.

12.3 Nazi control of Germany 1933–1945

LEARNING SUMMARY

After studying this section you will know:

- about the Nazi revolution in government
- how the Nazis kept control by propaganda and force
- how the Nazi state tried to purge itself of racial minorities and the disabled
- the effects of the Second World War on Nazi power

The Nazi revolution in government

AQA B
EDEXCEL A
OCR B
WJEC A   WJEC B
NICCEA

> The Reichstag tamely renewed the Enabling Act every four years.

> In 1938 General Blomberg, Defence Minister, and Werner von Fritsch, Commander in Chief, were removed from their posts along with over 100 other generals.

Hitler made himself a **dictator**. He demanded complete obedience to his will.

The forcible co-ordination of the state

After the Enabling Act of March 1933, Hitler was able to issue decrees. He alone was thought to understand what Germans really wanted. By the time Hindenburg died Hitler had transformed an ailing democracy into a dictatorship.

- The Reich Chancellery became the central institution of the state.
- The Cabinet faded into insignificance.
- Local government was destroyed.
- The civil service and judiciary accepted Nazi authoritarian rule.
- Only the army was a potential source of independent thought.
- Hitler took supreme command of a new High Command of the Armed Forces.

A one-party state

By 1940 there were 2 million full-time party officials. They formed an efficient network of control:

- **Gauleiter** was in charge of regions
- **Blockleiter** was in charge of 40–60 households

The structure of power

Hitler believed in the survival of the fittest. He expected state departments to compete for his favour. This resulted in chaos, not efficiency. He encouraged the overlapping of administrative responsibilities and rivalry between his key leaders, such as:

- **Rudolf Hess**, Hitler's deputy until 1941
- **Martin Bormann**, Chief of Staff to Hess from 1933–1941 and head of the Party Chancellery from 1941
- **Hans Heinrich Lammers**, Chief of the Reich Chancellery 1933–1945

Opposition to the Nazi regime

Most opposition was **passive**: grumbling and non-co-operation; refusing to join the Party; refusing to make the 'Heil Hitler' salute; telling anti-Hitler jokes. Resisters were:

For more information on the Gestapo and the SS see below.

- coerced by the Gestapo and the SS
- kept ignorant of events through control of the media

Unpopular policies were often moderated, most people's quibbles seemed minor and the Nazis had gained power through democracy.

Open opposition

Communists	*Rote Kapelle* smashed 1942
Workers	400 strikes 1933–1935
The Army	General Beck in 1938 von Stauffenburg in 1944
Youth Groups	Swing Youth Edelweiss Pirates White Rose Group
The Church	Martin Neimoller, Dietrich Bonhoeffer, Cardinal Galen

Examiner's tip: You need examples of each type of opposition.

It is estimated that 1.3 million Germans were put into concentration camps. A total of 300,000 left Germany from 1933–1939.

The destruction of opposition

AQA B
EDEXCEL A
OCR B
WJEC A   WJEC B
NICCEA

Totalitarianism demanded the active co-operation of many in the population.

Agencies of dictatorship

The Gestapo

- In 1933 **Heinrich Himmler** was put in charge of the Gestapo. Basic individual freedoms were removed and thousands of Germans were rounded up and sent to concentration camps. Courts were coerced so no authority could protect the population from the secret police.
- From 1936 it was the most important security agency, able to decide for itself what the law was.
- Its power was dependent on the consent and co-operation of ordinary German citizen.
- 80 per cent of investigations stemmed from voluntary denunciations.

The SS

- The **Schutzstaffel** began as Hitler's bodyguard, led by Himmler. From 280 members in 1929 it grew into a huge organisation. By the end of the 1930s it was involved in most aspects of the state.
- With the Gestapo, it was the most hated and repressive organisation of Nazi Germany.

Waffen-SS, the main branch, was primarily a military organisation.

The Deaths Head Formations administered the concentration camps and formed Panzer units. Later they organised the policy of mass extermination.

- The Emergency Power Decree of February 1933 allowed the SS to take suspects into 'protective custody'.
- By 1939 162,000 people were in 'protective custody' without trial and 225,000 had been imprisoned for political crimes.
- After the Night of the Long Knives the SS became the chief enforcement agency of the Nazi Party.
- By 1939 the 240,000 SS members were organised into the Waffen-SS and the Deaths Head Formations.

Was the Nazi State successful in destroying opposition?

The regime was certainly not able to repress all opposition, but most opposition was effectively deterred, and overt opposition was dealt with.

Propaganda and control

AQA B
EDEXCEL A
OCR B
WJEC A **WJEC B**
NICCEA

Probably the greatest propagandist of all time, he became the Reich Minister for Propaganda and Enlightenment in 1933 and became steadily more powerful in the Nazi state.

You need examples of each area of propaganda and control.

Propaganda

Much **culture** (art, architecture, music and literature) was conveyed to Germans through the mass media (newspapers, radio and film). The Nazi Government used culture and the mass media to spread **propaganda**, the point of view of the government, and to exclude differing opinions.

Josef Goebbels became Party propaganda chief in 1928.

Cultural control

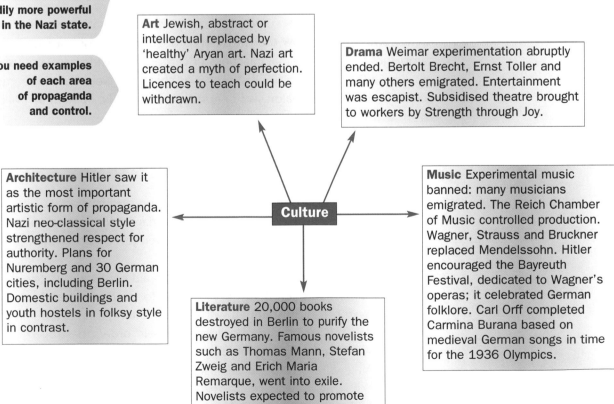

Art Jewish, abstract or intellectual replaced by 'healthy' Aryan art. Nazi art created a myth of perfection. Licences to teach could be withdrawn.

Drama Weimar experimentation abruptly ended. Bertolt Brecht, Ernst Toller and many others emigrated. Entertainment was escapist. Subsidised theatre brought to workers by Strength through Joy.

Architecture Hitler saw it as the most important artistic form of propaganda. Nazi neo-classical style strengthened respect for authority. Plans for Nuremberg and 30 German cities, including Berlin. Domestic buildings and youth hostels in folksy style in contrast.

Culture

Music Experimental music banned: many musicians emigrated. The Reich Chamber of Music controlled production. Wagner, Strauss and Bruckner replaced Mendelssohn. Hitler encouraged the Bayreuth Festival, dedicated to Wagner's operas; it celebrated German folklore. Carl Orff completed Carmina Burana based on medieval German songs in time for the 1936 Olympics.

Literature 20,000 books destroyed in Berlin to purify the new Germany. Famous novelists such as Thomas Mann, Stefan Zweig and Erich Maria Remarque, went into exile. Novelists expected to promote Nazi ideals or to be neutral.

Control of the mass media

The press	Rigorously controlled: editors made personally responsible for their papers. Nazi publishing house took over most papers.
Radio	The 'spiritual weapon of the totalitarian state'. Mass production of a cheap 'people's receiver' By 1939 70 per cent of households owned a radio. Mostly used for light entertainment, but transmitted Hitler's main speeches to estimated audience of 56 million.
Meetings and rallies	Atmosphere similar to pop concerts using light, uniforms, mass movements, stirring music striking flags and symbols. He made people wish to belong. 12 annual festivals, mass gym displays, Berlin Olympics etc.
Film	Mass entertainment; audiences quadrupled by 1942. **In 1942 all film companies were nationalised**. The Reich Film Chamber regulated the content of all films. Goebbels personally responsible. Most famous producer was Leni Riefenstahl.

The persecution of minorities

Nationalism held the state together. The Nazis believed in the superiority of the German race and thought they could only achieve victory and domination by purging the nation of weak groups. They thought this justified persecuting such groups:

> Aryan is the Nazi term for a non-Jewish German.

- **Gypsies**. They were considered non-Aryan and work shy. In 1935 intermarriage between gypsies and Aryans was banned. Many had already been sterilised as a result of a 1933 law. **From 1936 gypsies were sent to concentration camps** with other 'work-shy' tramps and beggars. From 1938 they had to be registered by the state. Many were sent to **Buchenwald** concentration camp. Only **5,000 gypsies (of 30,000 in Germany) survived the war**. In all about 500,000 European gypsies were exterminated from 1942–1945.
- **The mentally ill**. The Nazi policy of compulsory sterilisation was applied to them from 1933. In 1939 the Nazis began a 'euthanasia' or mass murder campaign. Starvation, lethal injections or carbon monoxide gas were used to murder 6,000 patients in the first year. Gas chambers were built in six mental hospitals, and the campaign was only stopped by public opinion in 1941. **By then about 72,000 people had been murdered**.
- **Jews**. They were persecuted from the beginning of Nazi rule.

Persecution of Jews

1933	Official boycott of Jewish shops, doctors and lawyers.
1935	The **Nuremberg Laws** banned marriages, forbade sexual relations between Jews and Aryans and removed Jewish citizenship.
1937	Jewish businesses were confiscated.
1938	All Jewish property was registered (to aid confiscation). Jewish doctors and dentists were forbidden to treat Aryans and Jewish passports were stamped with the red letter 'J'. In November came **Kristallnacht**: the SA, under Goebbels' orders, destroyed synagogues, Jewish homes and shops.
1939	All Jews forced to use the first names Sarah or Israel, and **emigration was promoted 'by every possible means'**. From 12 March 1939, the first mass arrests of Jews took place: 30,000 were sent to concentration camps.

The war turned mass persecution to genocide. Over 3 million Polish Jews had to be dealt with. It was impossible to do so by emigration.

- The first answer was to herd them together: **500,000 died in the Warsaw ghetto**, mostly from starvation and typhus. The invasion of Russia meant millions more Jews had to be dealt with.
- Special SS murder squads, **Einsatzgruppen**, killed 500,000 more in 1941.

> **KEY POINT**
> It is important to realise that extermination of the Jews was not even mentioned until 1939 and not agreed upon until 1941.

In early 1942 leading Nazis met at **Wannsee** in Berlin to work out a 'final solution'. **Death camps were built in Poland**. Here Jews and others were worked to death or gassed. Jews were moved from all over German-occupied Europe towards the Polish death camps. Some were used in hideous experiments. **Nearly 6 million Jews were killed, along with political opponents, homosexuals, Jehovah's Witnesses, 'anti-social elements', Russian prisoners of war and gypsies.**

Was Nazi Germany a totalitarian state?

AQA B
EDEXCEL A
OCR B
WJEC A   WJEC B
NICCEA

> **KEY POINT**
> A totalitarian state is a country where the government seeks to control all aspects of life to ensure that the people become committed members of the state.

The term 'totalitarian' does not mean complete control of all aspects of life and thought, rather the *wish* to control. The Nazi state was totalitarian in that it tried to force uniformity. There were practical limits to its control, however, as in any totalitarian state.

How much control was there?	How much freedom was there?
The power of the state in Nazi Germany was frightening:	The power of the state was limited:
• the SS and the Gestapo were not legally restrained in their use of power	• by the confusion of overlapping ministries
• Hitler's right to make law by decree was unlimited	• by the limited number of Gestapo personnel
• only the Nazi Party was tolerated	• above all by the need to rule with the consent and participation of the people
• through the complete control of information, culture and the mass media, the state tried to dictate even the thoughts of its citizens	
It is clear the Nazi state aimed to be totalitarian.	

PROGRESS CHECK

1. What Act gave Hitler the power to rule by decree?
2. Which three leaders vied with each other for Hitler's favour?
3. Name three army officers or groups who opposed Hitler.

1. The Enabling Act. 2. Rudolf Hess; Martin Bormann; Hans Heinrich Lammers 3. General Beck; von Stauffenberg; Army command at Kharkov.

12.4 Life in Nazi Germany

LEARNING SUMMARY

After studying this section you will know:

- how the Nazi government tried to influence and control young people
- how the Nazis tried to gain the confidence of women yet restrict their opportunities
- how the state promoted the family and divorce and prostitution
- how the economy was strengthened and weakened

Young people

AQA B
EDEXCEL A
OCR B
WJEC A   WJEC B
NICCEA

The Nazis wanted to completely indoctrinate German youth, from the time children were three years old. They used school and youth groups.

Nazi youth groups

Boys

- 6–10 **Pimpfen**: Cubs
- 10–14 **Deutsches Jungvolk**: Young German Boys
- 14–18 **Hitlerjugend**: Hitler Youth

Girls

- 10–24 **Jung Mädel**: Young Girls
- 14–18 **Bund Deutscher Mädel**: League of German Girls
- 18–21 **Glaube und Schönheit**: Faith and Beauty

Hitler Youth

> It became less successful as more uncommitted people joined.

This was founded in 1926 and expanded rapidly after 1933. **Baldur von Schirach** was appointed Nazi Youth Leader in 1931, aged 24.

After 1936 all other youth organisations were banned. Membership of Hitler Youth became compulsory, though many managed to avoid it.

Education

> Nazi ideas were particularly incorporated into biology and history. Physical exercise increased to at least two hours a day.

Nazi education taught that the state was more important than the individual. Under Nazi policies the state took over education:

- **National Socialist Teachers' League membership made almost compulsory for teachers**
- a **Nazi curriculum** was introduced.
- **higher education declined**, reflecting the Nazi downgrading of academic education
- **mixed schooling discouraged** to ensure the sexes received appropriate education: girls took needlework and music, language and home crafts.
- special schools established to train leaders. **National Political Institutes of Education** and **Adolf Hitler Schools** for boys aged 10–18 were set up. These were taken over by the SS in 1936, and provided a military-style boarding education. The best progressed to the **Ordensburgen** (Castles of Order). These castles housed 1,000 students aged 25–30 and 500 staff.

Women and the family

In 1933 Nazism was less popular among women than men. Nazism did become more popular among women in time, for complex reasons.

> Historians disagree as to whether women supported the Nazi regime more strongly than men.

Why Nazi policies attracted many women

- Nazis wanted to **reduce female employment** in industry and commerce.
- Marriage loans were given to women who gave up their jobs from 1933; men were preferred in the civil service.
- Nazis wanted to **increase the birth rate** of Aryan families.
- Nazi organisations supported the family by:
    - distributing food aid
    - giving medals to prolific mothers
    - providing maternity homes for the weeks after childbirth
    - running kindergartens to look after children while their mothers worked.
- The Nazi **Government did not dare force women out of employment from 1933-1939.**

> Women tended to be more conservative and hated violence. Many who did vote Nazi were attracted by promises to get Germany back onto its feet and to 'do social justice to the poor' by making sure that there was employment.

Success was limited

- 1933-1939 **birth rate rose slowly**, then declined. It never reached pre-1928 figures.
- **Nazi** racial and sterilisation **policies reduced the potential growth** of the population.
- During the war, **women were less mobilised than in Britain or the USA:**
    - Hitler refused female conscription
    - the government had to reverse previous policies and encourage female employment.

> Divorce became easier, to end unproductive marriages.

The economy and living standards

Most people voted Nazi in 1933 because of poverty. How far did the Nazis solve Germany's economic problems?

Jobs created

The Nazis created jobs by increasing government expenditure and investment.

- Hitler extended public works schemes (e.g. autobahns, housing).
- Hitler provided orders for private companies.
- Tax concessions to newlyweds stimulated demand.
- Trades unions were destroyed (industry benefited from cheap labour).
- Subsidies were given for hiring more workers.
- The civil service grew.
- Some groups were pressurised out of employment (e.g. women and Jews in the public service).

> Agricultural workers could not register for employment, so jobless figures for them were no longer kept. The Youth Service and conscription removed this age group from the jobless total.

Confidence increased

- **Hjalmar Schacht** was appointed Economics Minister in 1934 (inspired the confidence of financial institutions).
- **Brüning had ended reparations.**

Imports restricted

- **By 1934 imports were rising alarmingly**. Hitler agreed to Schacht's **New Plan, which regulated and reduced imports**. Schacht made agreements with other countries to provide strategic raw materials on an exchange or barter system. Even so, it was very difficult to keep down demand for foreign products.

Four-Year Plan created

- **Goering** (Commander of Luftwaffe) was put in charge of the Four-Year Plan in 1936.
- **The Four-Year Plan was to get Germany ready for war**. Targets were set for private industry. Germany was to be made self-sufficient (**autarkic**).

Production increased even more

- **Albert Speer** re-organised the economy for total war from 1942–1945. The invasion of Russia in 1941 had changed the nature of the conflict. Speer established a central planning board composed of industrialists and increased output enormously until 1945.

Success of Nazi policies in solving Germany's economic problems

Success	Failure
• Unemployment fell from 6 million to 1.6 million by 1936 • Germany recovered from the Depression very quickly	• Recovery had begun before 1933 • Other policies may have given faster, more sustained growth • Most Germans did not benefit greatly from economic growth • Autarky not achieved • Rearmament wasteful and disorganised until 1942 • The Third Reich did not achieve an above average growth rate in inter-war Europe

The German people under Nazi rule

AQA B
EDEXCEL A
OCR B
WJEC A   WJEC B
NICCEA

Did most people in Germany benefit from Nazi rule? This is impossible to answer since the evidence is so biased.

- Should we measure benefit with the eyes of people at the time or from our own point of view?
- How can the immoral persecution of minorities be balanced against the prosperity enjoyed by most Germans by 1939?
- Mass bombing, strains on the German economy and the Holocaust would have demanded a very different answer after 1939 from before.

PROGRESS CHECK

1. What were the two Nazi youth groups for boys and girls aged 14–18?
2. Why didn't many women support the Nazis early on?
3. Why didn't unemployed agricultural workers apear in Nazi unemployment statistics?

1. Hitler Youth; the League of German Girls. 2. Conservatism; dislike of violence. 3. Agricultural workers were not allowed to register for employment.

Sample GCSE questions

1.

(a) Name the two main groups that tried to take power from the Weimar Republic before the end of 1920. **(4)**

Keep these short: one mark for each group named, and one for developing it a little.

The Spartacists, who were communists, in March 1919 and the Freikorps in the Kapp Putsch in 1920.

(b) Why did the Nazi Party dislike the Weimar Republic 1921–23? **(6)**

The Nazi Party blamed the Weimar Republic for signing the Treaty of Versailles. In the 1923 Munich Putsch Hitler led a rebellion because the government was about to sign the Dawes Plan to make the payment of reparations possible.

Two good reasons are enough here, but explain each in its own short paragraph. The candidate has developed each of these sufficiently.

Hitler thought the Weimar Republic was weak because it was democratic and no party could gain a majority in the Reichstag without a coalition.

(c) 'The most important reason why the Weimar Republic was weak was the unfairness of the Treaty of Versailles' Do you agree with this statement? Explain your answer. **(10)**

The Treaty of Versailles was not the only reason for the weakness of the Weimar Republic before 1929. In many ways Germany had brought weakness on herself, rather than having it imposed on her. The loss of the war, the abdication of the Kaiser, the creation of the weak Republican Constitution and the extremism of German politics would have made Germany weak even without the Treaty.

The question spans the whole period from 1919–1933. There are two periods of weakness and two arguments – for and against Versailles. Versailles is the main reason.

However, the Treaty did shock the German nation. The loss of so many Germans to other states, such as Poland, was an important reason for nationalists like Kapp and Hitler to blame the government. The restrictions on German armed forces, especially the army, meant that the Republic could not police itself properly.

Communism was bred by poverty, which in turn was prolonged at least by the need to pay the reparations demanded by the Treaty.

For high marks you need to include a little detail to show that you know the period adequately. It is most important to include reasons. This candidate has come to a definite conclusion.

After 1929, the determination of Hindenburg to rule by decree was important, but the Wall Street Crash and the effects of the Depression on Germany were important too.

The fact that the Depression hit Germany so hard was because of the web of loans set up to allow the payment of reparations, e.g. the Young Plan. Hitler was also able to profit by promising to destroy the Treaty of Versailles: nationalism was the cement that bound the Nazi Party together.

So, though Germany would have been weak without the Versailles Treaty, the Treaty was probably the most important cause of its weakness.

The USA 1919–1941

The following topic is covered in this chapter:

● Boom and slump in the USA 1919-41

13.1 Boom and slump in the USA 1919–1941

LEARNING SUMMARY

After studying this section you will know:

● how the USA isolated itself from alliances and the world economy
● the boom of the 1920s
● the crisis on Wall Street and how it affected the whole of American society
● how President Hoover failed to pull the USA out of the crisis
● how Roosevelt turned the tide with the New Deal

The growth of isolation 1919–1922

AQA B
EDEXCEL A
OCR B
WJEC A
NICCEA

Woodrow Wilson (Democrat) President 1913–1921

1914–1918　**The USA had profited** hugely by supplying food, war and consumer goods to Europe.

1919　At the Paris Peace Conference, Wilson had a formative influence on the Treaty of Versailles and the formation of the League of Nations. However, **Congress refused to agree to the Treaty or join the League**.

> Congress was now Republican. Wilson became ill trying to change its mind.

Warren Harding (Republican) President 1921–1923

1922　He organised the **Fordney–McCumber Tariff**. It taxed imports from foreign countries. At first it protected American farming and industry. Later, foreign countries kept out American goods.

During the inter-war years the USA tried to steer clear of entanglements abroad and to promote peace and disarmament.

The boom of the 1920s

AQA B
EDEXCEL A
OCR B
WJEC A
NICCEA

KEY POINT　In a boom, products are in demand. Industry thrives and unemployment falls.

The economy grew quickly during the 1920s because:

● profits from the war and huge resources were used to create new industries
● at first there was little competition from European industry and farming

Consumers could borrow easily in order to buy.

People spent their savings, invested in industries, were lent money easily.

This stimulated huge growth in the glass, rubber and steel industries.

- a growing population was further increased by immigration
- republican policies cut taxes on profits and industry
- technological change, especially mass production, worked in America's favour
- there was a huge expansion of credit
- confidence in America was high

Growth industries

The motor industry – Private car ownership grew from 9 to 26 million from 1919–1929. Ford's Detroit plant produced one car every three minutes using the **production line**. It paid its workers $5 a day.

You need to remember some examples of growing industries. Two or three will do.

Mass media – Radios became common: from 60,000 in 1919 to 10 million in 1929. The film industry grew. Attendance more than doubled.

Transport – The mileage of paved road doubled. The number of trucks tripled. Railways declined, but civil aviation grew from nothing to over 150,000 flights by 1929.

Communications – There were 20 million telephones by 1929.

Consumer good – Refrigerators began to appear. Vacuum cleaners became popular. These changes were stimulated by mass advertising, chain stores, easy delivery and hire purchase.

Changes in US society during the 1920s

AQA B
EDEXCEL A
OCR B
WJEC A
NICCEA

Mass production, mass marketing, easier communications and increasing wealth changed some parts of society during the 1920s.

The Roaring '20s

- Women became more emancipated: they wore short skirts and vampish make-up, and had jobs in offices.
- The motor car widened people's horizons. It made day trips, holidays, commuting and shopping much easier.
- Radio began in 1920 and by 1930 40 per cent of homes had one. New ideas spread much more quickly and popular music was born.
- Clubs and dancing became popular in towns.
- Jazz became popular. It moved from a black audience to general acceptance among the young.
- Sexual conventions loosened. Sex outside marriage became more common.
- The cinema affected everyone: everyone wanted to live like the stars (Rudolf Valentino, Clara Bow, Theda Bara).

BUT

Which of these restricted the buying power of the home market? These are the ones you need to remember.

- Some industries declined: cotton, coal, tin and copper.
- Blacks as a whole were unable to enjoy the boom. they were isolated in rural or urban poverty.
- Agriculture declined gradually through oversupply and low prices.
- There was general fear of communism, caused by strikes and bombs. This led to the Palmer Raids.
- Prohibition (the Volstead Act) produced lawlessness.
- The Ku Klux Klan aimed to keep rural blacks poor.
- There was discrimination against immigrants, e.g. the Sacco and Vanzetti trial.

Causes and consequences of the Wall Street Crash

AQA B
EDEXCEL A
OCR B
WJEC A
NICCEA

> **Buying 'on the margin' meant that investors borrowed 90% of the cost of shares from banks.**

> **Examiner's tip:** You will not be examined on details of the crash itself, but it is useful to remember that speculation had assisted in the rise of the market and accelerated its fall.

- By 1929 agriculture was in decline.
- Industry was suffering from foreign competition and tariffs, and the failure of the domestic market to grow fast enough.
- The long boom on the Wall Street Stock Exchange came to an end: investors who had raised money 'on the margin' now realised that share and stock prices would not continue to rise since industry expected lower profits. Instead of buying, they sold at a loss.

The Wall Street Crash

Over about 10 days in late October 1929 the Wall Street Stock exchange crashed.

The worst days were:

- 'Black Thursday' (24 October) when nearly 13 million shares were sold
- Tuesday (29 October) when over 16 million shares were sold

Stocks and shares had become worthless.

The result of the Wall Street Crash

- Banks that had lent money to investors 'on the margin' lost huge amounts. Over 5,000 closed from 1930–1933.
- Industry suffered when shares became worthless and consumers stopped buying goods (many were taken over or shut down).
  Farming suffered. Less food was bought (there was already a surplus) so prices fell. Farmers could not invest in fertilisers and worsened the 'Dust Bowl' problem (over-worked farmland turned to dust).
- Farmers and businesses went out of business. Unemployment rose from 1.6 to 14 million by 1933.
- Consumers lost their money in the banks and suffered as interest rates rose. Many became homeless and destitute and lived in '**Hoovervilles**' (shanty towns).

 KEY POINT

> In a slump there is oversupply of products and not enough money to buy them. Unemployment rises. When it seems impossible to climb out of the slump, it is called a depression.

Government reaction and recovery attempts 1929–1933

AQA B
EDEXCEL A
OCR B
WJEC A
NICCEA

Herbert Hoover (Republican) President 1929–1933

In 1928 Hoover had promised '**two cars in every garage and a chicken in the pot**'.

He thought **the economy should be left to right itself**. As the Depression grew, however, he was forced into several actions.

- The **Smoot–Hawley Tariff 1930**. This increased import taxes as high as 50 per cent to encourage people to buy American goods. They could not afford to buy anyway.

Few governments would have reacted well to the Wall Street Crash and the beginning of the Depression. However, voters became bitter about Hoover's failure because he did not appear to care for the individuals caught in poverty.

- The **Hoover Dam** and other construction projects cost the government $423 million. They were a small step in the right direction.
- **The Farm Board bought up surplus farm produce**, but could not buy enough to make a difference.
- **The Reconstruction Finance Corporation 1932** provided $1,500 million in loans to big business.

Hoover relied on voluntary agreements with industrialists to keep prices up. He refused to provide relief for the hungry and homeless.

State governments and charity were not enough help in this catastrophic situation. The results were:

MacArthur met them with tanks.

- increasing numbers of **strikes and lockouts**
- a march on Washington by First World War veterans (**The Bonus Marchers**) in 1932 – they were demanding the pension due in 1945
- spreading poverty and starvation
- Hoovervilles were common

The crisis came to a head during the presidential election of 1932.

The 1932 Presidential election

AQA B
EDEXCEL A
OCR B
WJEC A
NICCEA

Herbert Hoover: Republican

- Businesses would bring prosperity **without government interference**.
- **Relief** should be provided **by the individual state governments and charity**.
- Thought to be cold and detached: **'In Hoover we trusted and now we are busted'**.

Franklin D. Roosevelt: Democrat

- **Promised government schemes** to provide jobs and revive industry and agriculture.
- Promised **federal aid to the poor and unemployed**.
- Promised **protection for workers. from employers**.
- Promised to **end Prohibition**.
- **Understood** that the poor needed help.

The election was a landslide victory for Roosevelt, with a **7 million majority**.

The New Deal

AQA B
EDEXCEL A
OCR B
WJEC A
NICCEA

Roosevelt's contribution

In 1933 Roosevelt became President. His inaugural speech:

'…was one of the turning points of American history. In a few minutes Roosevelt did what had so wearyingly eluded Hoover for four years: he gave back to his countrymen their hope and their energy…'

(Hugh Brogan, *History of the United States of America*, 1985)

In contrast to Hoover, Roosevelt did appear to care. He inspired confidence in the financial markets and among the poor. Confidence was important in restoring normality on the Stock Exchange and in financial life generally.

Roosevelt said:

'...the only thing we have to fear is fear itself – nameless, unreasoning, unjustified terror which paralyses needed efforts to convert retreat into advance ...'

Roosevelt promised:

- **relief** of poverty – to stop people losing jobs and farms, and to feed the starving
- **recovery** of industry– to get everyone working again
- **reform** – to provide unemployment insurance, old age pensions and to help the sick

- Roosevelt **spoke directly to the people in 'fireside chats'**, the first only eight days after taking office.
- He brought together a group of people (the Brain Trust) to decide on specific measures that needed to be taken. He was sure of the general direction needed.

Congress was so alarmed at the state of the country that it was prepared to give him emergency powers.

- **He persuaded the country that he would take measures irrespective of party or class loyalties.**
- He put the **whole resources of government into the creation of the New Deal programme**.

Fig. 13.1 An anti-Roosevelt cartoon, March 1933.

The First Hundred Days

In 1933 Roosevelt:

- shut all the banks for a 'four-day holiday'. Their books were checked and the government decided which were safe to re-open. This restored confidence so money flowed into banks again.
- ended Prohibition. This deprived organised crime of its profits and allowed the alcohol industry to be taxed again.
- created the '**Alphabet Agencies**'. These provided employment and support.

Fig. 13.2 Cartoon Roosevelt making a new start, March 1933.

The Alphabet Agencies

Farm Credit Administration (FCA)	Made loans to farmers so they were financially secure.
Agricultural Adjustment Agency (AAA)	Paid farmers to produce less food so prices went up.
Civilian Conservation Corps (CCC)	Gave conservation work to young men. This took them out of the job market and gave them worthwhile jobs to do: planting trees to anchor soil and providing flood control.
Civilian Works Administration (CWA)	This was an emergency measure to get through the first winter. The agency tried to employ as many as possible, clearing leaves, building roads etc.
Public Works Administration (PWA)	Spent $7 billion on lasting public works: buildings, bridges, sewerage, dams etc.
Federal Emergency Relief Administration (FERA)	Spent $500 million on soup kitchens, clothing, schools and employment schemes.
Home Owners' Loan Corporation (HOLC)	Lent money to stop people losing their homes.
National Recovery Administration (NRA)	Aimed to increase wages and prices and give workers a fairer deal. Employers had to sign a code for their own industry and were then allowed to display the NRA Blue Eagle.
The Tennessee Valley Authority (TVA)	Aimed to improve the vast Tennessee Valley: by building 33 dams, improving the soil, planting forests and improving river communications. As a by-product it provided hydro-electricity.

These measures put new heart into the American people. The measures began to regenerate trust and confidence and begin the long journey back to prosperity.

How the New Deal changed after 1933

AQA B
EDEXCEL A
OCR B
WJEC A
NICCEA

Roosevelt had never been sure of the details of what would be needed, so after the Hundred Days there were more measures.

The **Works Progress Administration 1935** (WPA)	Provided work on roads, public buildings, schools, bridges, tunnels, sewers and erosion control.
The **Social Security Act 1935**	Gave a state pension to everyone over 65, supported handicapped people and mothers with young children, and helped to provide unemployment insurance.
The **Wagner Act 1935**	Gave freedom to form unions and prevented employers from sacking trades union members.
The **Resettlement Administration 1935**	Helped to resettle unemployed sharecroppers, tenants and farmworkers. In 1937 this was replaced by the **Farm Security Agency**, which gave loans to sharecroppers and tenant farmers to buy their own land.

Opposition to the New Deal

AQA B
EDEXCEL A
OCR B
WJEC A
NICCEA

Fig. 13.3 'Priming the Pump': an American view in 1933.

Republicans

Republicans opposed Roosevelt because:

- many thought paying money to the unemployed would make them lazy
- they thought **money was being wasted**
- they resented the higher taxation that was needed
- **they accused Roosevelt of communism** because he had taken so much power to solve the crisis
- they doubted that he had the right to dictate to business

Business

Business thought like Republicans, but also:

- was angry at Roosevelt's support for trades unions
- thought the TVA competed unfairly with privately owned businesses

The rich

Resented having to pay high taxes.

Huey Long, Governor of Louisiana

Long wanted to increase taxes on the rich. He proposed:

- to redistribute wealth over $5000 in his 'Share Our Wealth' scheme
- a minimum wage etc.

Huey Long was assassinated.

The Supreme Court

- In 1935 the Supreme Court decided the NRA was unconstitutional because the government could not control businesses.
- In 1936 it declared the measures taken by the AAA were unconstitutional because agriculture could only be regulated by state governments.

A win for Roosevelt

However, in the 1936 presidential election Roosevelt won with an astounding 27 million votes. Only 16 million voted Republican.

Roosevelt then **attacked the Supreme Court** by trying to appoint six new judges to gain a majority there.

Even his own supporters thought that he had gone too far. He was forced to back down but the Supreme Court moderated its opposition.

Further depression hit the economy in 1937, and by 1939 Roosevelt admitted that the New Deal was over.

Failure of the New Deal

Many parts of American society were hardly touched by the New Deal.

Blacks

They continued to suffer severe discrimination. They were prohibited from living in areas around the TVA dams.

They found it very hard to find jobs. By 1935, about 30 per cent lived on relief.

Roosevelt depended on southern, white, Democratic Congressmen for his political support. They would not support civil rights or anti-lynching laws.

However, black people did benefit from the CCC programme and new housing built after slum-clearance projects. Some gained jobs in the administration.

Women

> White men benefited most from the New Deal.

Women were not employed to any great degree in the manual labour programmes, but their employment rose during the 1930s because they provided cheap labour. They benefited to some extent from the Social Security Act. Some, like Mary Macleod Bethume (head of NYA) and Frances Perkins (Secretary of Labour), rose to prominent positions in the administration.

Recovery and success of the New Deal to 1941

AQA B
EDEXCEL A
OCR B
WJEC A
NICCEA

Everyone agrees that the New Deal was very important but historians disagree about how important it was in promoting recovery.

Successes

- The New Deal was successful in reviving businesses and reducing unemployment.
- **It stopped the situation getting worse and communism spreading**.
- It **provided relief** for those who could no longer help themselves.

Failures

- It cost **billions of dollars of** Government money but failed permanently to solve the problem.
- When the government reduced its support in 1937, **unemployment rose steeply again**.
- Continual **support remained necessary** until, in 1941, the Second World War provided work for all.
- Some parts of society benefited more than others.

PROGRESS CHECK

1. Give three examples of consumer products that were popular in the 1920s.
2. Name three industries that did not enjoy a boom in the mid-1920s.
3. Which two Alphabet Agencies helped farmers?

1. Radios, refrigerators, vacuum cleaners. 2. Choose from: cotton, tin, coal, copper, farming. 3. FCA and AAA.

Exam practice questions

1.

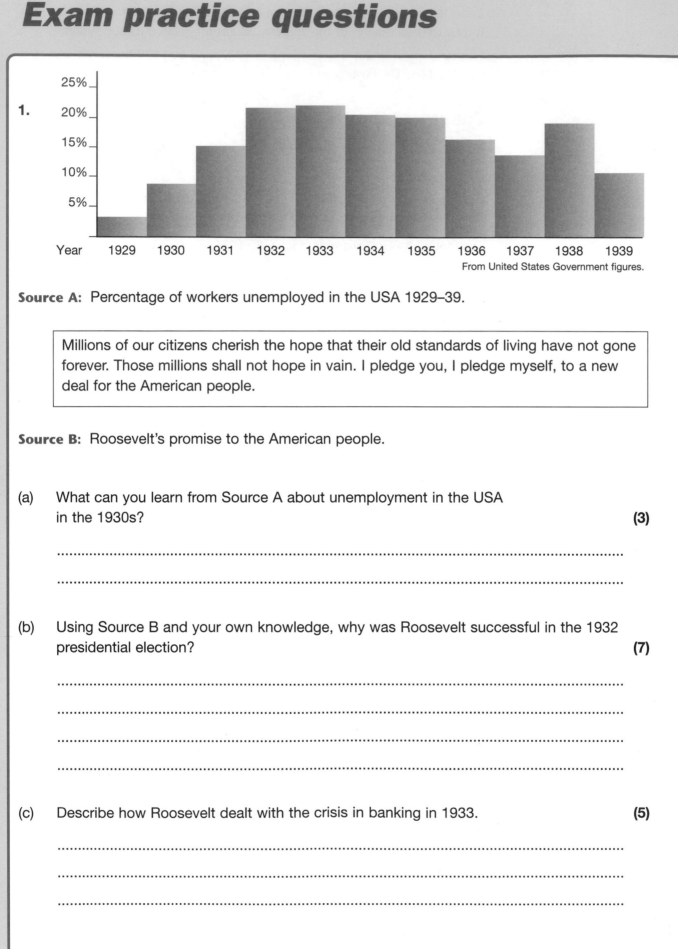

Source A: Percentage of workers unemployed in the USA 1929–39.

> Millions of our citizens cherish the hope that their old standards of living have not gone forever. Those millions shall not hope in vain. I pledge you, I pledge myself, to a new deal for the American people.

Source B: Roosevelt's promise to the American people.

(a) What can you learn from Source A about unemployment in the USA in the 1930s? **(3)**

....

....

(b) Using Source B and your own knowledge, why was Roosevelt successful in the 1932 presidential election? **(7)**

....

....

....

....

(c) Describe how Roosevelt dealt with the crisis in banking in 1933. **(5)**

....

....

....

Exam practice questions

EITHER

(d) Did the New Deal end the Depression in the USA in the 1930s? Explain your answer. **(15)**

....
....
....
....
....
....
....
....
....
....
....
....

OR

(e) Why had the USA fallen into depression in 1929? **(15)**

....
....
....
....
....
....
....
....
....
....
....
....

AQA Specimen Paper 2

Exam practice answers

Chapter 2

1.

(a) Source A tells us they are pleased the war is starting because they are cheering. A lot of people are pictured, so many people welcomed the war.

(b) Posters like the one in Source B partly explain why men joined the army. The poster is appealing to their sense of loyalty and duty to their country. Other posters did this as well. They made men feel they were cowards if they did not volunteer. Kitchener organised a massive recruiting campaign and there were posters like this one all over the country.

However, there were other reasons why men volunteered. The start of the war was very popular. Everyone thought that Britain ought to defend Belgium against the might of Germany. Germany was unpopular in Britain because it was Britain's rival. So most men did not need to be encouraged to volunteer. They felt it was the right thing to do. They also thought the war would be over by Christmas, so they did not mind being away for just a few months.

(c) This source is useful in explaining why the British casualties at the Somme were so high. The source mentions that the British soldiers were walking along casually, looking as if they did not expect to see anything alive. The British artillery had bombarded the German trenches before the attack to knock out all the German front-line trenches. This was why the British soldiers were not expecting to find any opposition. The bombardment had not worked, however. The Germans were dug in so deep they survived it. The source tells us they were able to put their machine guns in place after the bombardment. The bombardment also let the Germans know a major attack was about to take place. This is why they were ready for the British soldiers, who were taken by surprise. This explains why so many soldiers were killed.

(d) This might not be a completely fair interpretation because it was written in a newspaper to commemorate the outbreak of the First World War. This might mean that the author is going to be sympathetic to the ordinary soldiers because so many of them died. Some of his language shows this: he uses words like 'gallantly' to describe the soldiers, but he puts the blame on the generals.

However, it is not fair to blame the generals for all the deaths. Trench warfare was something new and no one at the time knew the right way to fight such a war. Weapons of defence like machine guns were much more effective than attacking weapons like the tanks, many of which got stuck in the mud. No one knew how to break through the enemy trenches. The generals kept on ordering the men to charge over the top. They were mowed down by the machine guns. Perhaps the generals should have tried different tactics but they should not bear all the blame; they were just trying to win the war.

Chapter 4

1.

(a) The main aims were to prevent war by settling disputes peacefully through the League, to encourage disarmament and to improve working conditions around the world.

(b) America did not join the League because many Americans were isolationists. They thought that countries in Europe were always quarrelling and they did not want to get dragged into these quarrels. They had already lost a lot of men in the First World War and they did not want more Americans dying. They thought America could do well if it kept itself to itself. They also thought that getting involved in the League would be expensive because America was the richest country in the world and would end up paying for everything. Germany was not allowed to join as a punishment for starting the war. Many people were afraid Germany would cause more trouble and thought Germany should be kept weak and not treated as an equal. Only when it had shown that it could behave properly would it be treated as an equal.

(c) There were several reasons why the League was weak in the 1920s. The lack of an army was certainly one, but others include the fact that the USA was not a member, the way the League was organised, and the fact that the main countries in the League were not ready to stand up to powerful countries. It is important to remember that the League was able to put together armed forces to back up its decisions if economic sanctions did not work. However, the League never came close to putting such an army together. This was because of the lack of will of countries like France and Britain to use force to sort out problems. They were afraid of starting another war and still remembered how dreadful the First World War had been. This explains why the League failed to stand up to a powerful country like Italy in the crisis over Corfu. Italy invaded Corfu and the League failed to act. It was left to the Conference of Ambassadors to deal with the problem. Mussolini simply threatened to leave the League if it acted against him.

However, in other crises like the one over the Aaland Islands, the League did set up a Commission of Enquiry and did solve the dispute. However, this was only between Finland and Sweden – two weak countries. So even if the League had an army it probably would not have used it.

There were many other reasons why the League was weak. The fact that the USA did not join meant that the League lost a lot of authority. The League was also very slow to act because its decisions had to be unanimous and this took a long time to achieve and often ended in a compromise being reached. Another problem was that most member countries were more concerned about their own self-interest than about international justice. An example of this was in 1923 when France invaded the Ruhr because Germany was getting behind with reparation payments. This invasion was illegal but the League did nothing about it because France was one of its leading members.

In conclusion, the League's lack of an army was not as important as its lack of will and the self-interest of its members. While these existed, an army would not be much use.

Chapter 7

1.

(a) Delegates agreed at Potsdam that Germans in Eastern Europe were to be sent back to Germany. This resulted in millions of refugees streaming across Europe. They also agreed the Polish–German frontier and reparations for the Allies.

(b) The USA introduced the Marshall Plan to help the economies of the Western European countries recover. France's economy had been destroyed by Germany's occupation, and Britain was exhausted by the war effort. The USA spent billions of dollars to help these economies recover.

America also had political reasons for doing this. Americans were afraid communist ideas would thrive in countries that were poor. The Marshall Plan was aimed at stopping communism spreading into Western Europe. America also gained some control over Western Europe by making those economies so dependent on her. The last reason was that the countries being helped had to agree to buy American goods and this led to an economic boom in America. So America's economy was helped as well.

(c) There were several reasons for the Cold War. The USA and the USSR represented different political systems and beliefs. Russia was communist and regarded capitalism as evil. America believed in democracy and thought that communism was anti-democratic and against freedom. So the two powers were bound to come into conflict because of their beliefs.

However, this was made worse by the distrust between the two countries. Both thought that the other was planning to take over Europe and even the rest of the world. Both made moves that were defensive, e.g. Russia wanted a barrier between itself and Western Europe. But such moves were regarded as aggressive by the other side because of the lack of trust. This was also to be found in the relationship between the leaders. When Roosevelt had been President of the USA, he had got on with Stalin quite well. But he was replaced by Truman who was much more suspicious of Stalin and Russia. He was sure Stalin wanted to make all Europe communist. Stalin did not trust Truman. His distrust was made worse when he discovered the existence of America's atom bomb, which was kept a secret for a long time.

The suspicion between Truman and Stalin was important but was only one of a number of factors and it was simply an extension of the general suspicion between the two countries. This means it is difficult to say that one cause was the most important because they were all connected.

Chapter 9

1.

(a) This speech gave hope to these people because Khrushchev had taken over as leader of Russia after Stalin died in 1953. Stalin had a very harsh policy towards countries in Eastern Europe. He gave them no freedom and used them merely to protect the Soviet Union. In the speech Khrushchev mentions Stalin using terror and behaving like a criminal towards foreign countries. Khrushchev's speech suggests he is going to change Stalin's policies. One of the first things Khrushchev did was to improve relations with Tito in Yugoslavia. He assured Yugoslavia that he believed in non-interference and national independence.

(b) The cartoonist is trying to say that Russia was trying to keep control of Eastern Europe. This is shown by the fact that Khrushchev has a whip and has most of the countries behaving on their stands. They are also inside his cage. However, the bear representing Yugoslavia is shown off the stand. This is because Tito had made Yugoslavia an independent communist country free of control by the Soviet Union. Hungary is shown getting off the stand: this shows the uprising in Hungary which took place in 1956. So the cartoonist is saying that Soviet control is breaking down in places.

(c) I do not completely believe this source. Gero had only been in charge of Hungary for a few months. Also the author is biased against him. We can see that by what he says about him only smiling when he ordered demonstrators to be shot. The author did take part in the revolution so he will be against Gero. Hungarians did not like Gero – they thought he was just another person put there by Russia – but there were other reasons for the revolution like the death of Stalin and the speech by Khrushchev in Source A which raised people's hopes. They also thought that America would help them if they rebelled against Soviet control.

Chapter 11

1.

(a) Collectivisation was the clearing of peasant farms and the uniting of the land-holdings into large farms on which the ex-peasants would work as labourers under Communist Party managers.

(b) NEP had collapsed in 1928, but in any case the communists expected to industrialise and create a larger industrial working class. They wanted heavy industry to provide guns and tanks for defence, and they wanted to be strong compared to their industrial competitors abroad. Stalin said that the Soviet Union was 50 years behind the Western nations, and that they should make it up in ten, otherwise they would go under.

(c) If I were a peasant, then the changes in farming would be most important to me. They affected most of the USSR, most quickly. They involved the total remodelling of the agricultural landscape. They involved the loss of economic freedom by the individual peasant, forced into the closely controlled collective. They were called 'a coup d'etat against the peasantry' by Prof. Moishe Lewin, because they destroyed peasant political power, as well as their ability to refuse to supply industrial towns with their produce. The communist leadership was incontestably in charge in the countryside, and they were able to decide where the food went. Perhaps 10 million people died in the Ukraine and the Caucasus in 1932-1933 so that their corn could be exported to earn foreign currency to spend on industrial machinery. Economically, collectivisation was a failure in that it did not produce quick increases in yields, and was only beginning to improve output by the late 1930s, after an initially catastrophic reduction.

If I were a worker I would be most impressed by the changes in industry: the huge increases in output of iron, steel and coal; the building of huge factories, such as at Stalingrad; dams, such as the Dneipr; electrification and improvements in rail and canal transport. By 1940, industrial output had increased 15 times over that of 1913 and about 10 times that of 1928. Unemployment had disappeared, towns had doubled in size and industry had become more important than farming for the first time. As a worker, my standard of living may not have improved much, because of the housing shortage and the fear of political purges and accusations of sabotage, but the country had been transformed.

Changes both in agriculture and industry were very important in the 1930s, but the changes in industry were more immediately successful, and were clearly thought more important by Stalin's government. It was the huge increase in industrial capacity that allowed the Soviet Union to defeat Hitler during the Second World War, so that the importance of the Five-Year Plans cannot be overestimated.

Chapter 13

1.

(a) Unemployment in the USA soared from 3.2 per cent in 1929 to 24.9 per cent in 1933 and had not returned to its original low figure by 1939, when there were still 11.2 per cent unemployed. While it is obvious that, after the introduction of the New Deal in 1933, there was a general trend downwards for unemployment, it actually increased in 1938, and by 1939 Roosevelt's policies had not been wholly successful.

(b) Between 1929 and 1932, Hoover's policies had been unsuccessful because he did not spend sufficient money early enough and he did not commit the whole nation to war against depression, deceit and despair, as Roosevelt would. In his speech in 1932, Roosevelt was committing himself. He said: 'I pledge you, I pledge myself, to a New Deal for the American people.' This meant that he would involve the federal government as never before. Later he said that he would declare war on the problem. It should also be pointed out that he was involving the whole nation in this crusade. So the reason for his success was not just that he followed the failure of Hoover, but that he promised a new kind of commitment to the American people.

(c) The problem with the banks was that no one trusted them any more, so Roosevelt's leadership in, for example, his inauguration speech and his fireside chats was very important. He didn't just say that the government would take measures, he told the people to help too, by putting their money back into the banks. Most practically, as soon as he became president, Roosevelt closed the banks in a four-day 'bank holiday' and made them prove that they were safe before they started trading again. He also spent government money to stop more going bankrupt. Many of his other measures helped depositors, so they could pay off their debts to the banks, such as the Farm Credit Association and the Home Owners' Loan Corporation. Just making the economy work again would have the effect of improving the profitability of banking.

EITHER

(d) Source A shows that the New Deal had not reduced unemployment to the 1929 figure by the end of 1939, but it suggests that overall the unemployment figure did drop from 1933 onwards. It seems that the New Deal had been successful, but there are several other factors to take into account.

It cannot be proved that unemployment would not have fallen even without the New Deal, as it did, for example, in Germany and Great Britain. They both took measures to improve the situation, but did not attack the problem as expensively as the USA. By raising so much extra money in taxation, Roosevelt may actually have harmed the long-term prospects for the recovery of the US economy. It is also true to say that the impact of Roosevelt's measures was very uneven. Blacks continued to suffer, so that by 1935 30 per cent lived on relief. While several women rose to prominent positions in the administration, most remained unemployed. So the New Deal was certainly not wholly successful in ending depression in the USA.

Of course most people agree that the New Deal achieved a very great improvement, both in the morale of the American people and in the standard of living of the poorest Americans. While it did not solve the problem, it did preserve the USA from sinking lower into poverty and perhaps even from revolution. The Alphabet Agencies were like a lifebelt thrown to the American people. They worked best in the short term, but how effective they may have been in the longer term we shall never know because the opposition of the Supreme Court, the Republicans and business helped to destroy some measures (the NRA) and reduce the effectiveness of others. By 1938 Roosevelt was forced to almost bring the New Deal to a halt. So, while the New Deal did not end the depression, it certainly did a lot of good in the first few years.

OR

(e) There had been a remarkable increase in American prosperity, especially because of the First World War. They were not very involved in the war itself until the last year and they profited hugely because they could supply a world market when others could not. This prosperity carried through into the early 1920s, but by then their competitors throughout the world were able to begin to win back their markets, and some industries began to suffer. In 1922, President Warren Harding imposed the Fordney–McCumber Tariff, which at first improved the situation, protecting American markets from competition. Unfortunately other countries began to put taxes on American goods in reprisal, so that in the long run it worsened the American position. Cotton, tin, copper and coal joined the slow decline of farming due to oversupply. So depression was gathering in the 1920s even before the Wall Street Crash.

But depression was not just because of foreign competition. At home the Americans had failed to spread the wealth through society, so that many were unable to consume in even reasonable quantities. Black people as a whole were too poor to buy radios, refrigerators and motor cars. Most farmers were becoming poorer. By the late 1920s, most industrial workers were finding jobs hard to keep. With hindsight, what is surprising is that, in its feverish buying of shares, Wall Street took so long to recognise that companies were no longer profitable as they once had been. When the Crash came, it was a belated and severe correction to the speculation that had marked the late 1920s. Buying on the margin involved a much wider selection of the public than would normally have been involved and, fatally, it involved banks in the destruction of 1920s prosperity.

Index